Maine 101

Everything you wanted to know about Maine and were going to ask anyway

Nancy Griffin

MACINTYRE PURCELL PUBLISHING INC.

MacIntyre Purcell Publishing Inc.
194 Hospital Rd.
Lunenburg, Nova Scotia
B0J 2C0
(902) 640-2337
www.macintyrepurcell.com
info@macintyrepurcell.com

Cover photo courtesy of iStock.
Photos: iStock.
Printed and bound in Canada by Marquis.
Map courtesy of MaineDOT.
Design and layout: Channel Communications

Library and Archives Canada Cataloguing in Publication

Griffin, Nancy
    Maine 101 : everything you wanted to know about Maine
and were going to ask anyway / Nancy Griffin. -- 2nd ed.

(101 series)
Also issued in electronic format.
ISBN 978-1-927097-31-1

    1. Maine. 2. Maine--Miscellanea. I. Title.

F17.3.G74 2012   974.1   C2012-906134-4

We acknowledge the financial support of the Government of Canada through Department of Canadian Heritage (Canada Book Fund) and the Nova Scotia Department of Tourism, Culture and Heritage.

Introduction

It comes as no surprise to Mainers that there is a genuine soft spot for the state throughout the country. It may have something to do with the old values and courtesies that seem to be disappearing from an increasingly urban America. It also has something to do with Mainers resilience in the face of tough economic conditions and sometimes furious weather. Whatever it is, it is immediately recognizable, and it is an identity like no other.

As we will see, Maine is rural and urban, rich and poor, a playground for the wealthy, and sometimes struggling with visions for itself in the future. Maine is like interesting places everywhere; a product of contradictions, and it was our duty and pleasure to include as many of them as we could, drawing what we hope is a multi-faceted portrait revealed in tiny increments, one fact or story at a time.

No one book can really be about everything, of course. As you might expect, our toughest decisions were not what to put in but what to leave out. For every tidbit or profile or anecdote that didn't survive the final trimming, we gave a collective sigh of sorrow and crossed our fingers that it would make the next edition.

As you might expect, *Maine 101* could not have been written without dozens of collaborators and supporters, and so there are a great many people to thank. At the top of the list are the friends, researchers, and librarians without whose support this book might not have happened. Also a special thank you to John MacIntyre and Kelly Inglis at the home office for their direction and help in the development of the final manuscript.

Others who contributed include Stephanie Philbrick and Richard Shaw. Finally, our gratitude goes to those whose personal takes on this great State were shoehorned into lists of five at our request — their thoughts and their willingness to share them truly helped us make this book unique.

-Nancy Griffin

Table of Contents

State of Maine Song

Written and composed by Roger Vinton Snow (1890-1952)

Grand State of Maine, proudly we sing

To tell your glories to the land

To shout your praises till the echoes ring

Should fate unkind send us to roam

The scent of the fragrant pines,

The tang of the salty sea will call us home.

Oh, Pine Tree State

Your woods, fields and hills

Your lakes, streams and rockbound coast

Will ever fill our hearts with thrills

And tho' we seek far and wide

Our search will be in vain

To find a fairer spot on earth

Than Maine! Maine! Maine!

Maine:

A Timeline

21,000 years before present: The Laurentide ice sheet begins retreating from the Gulf of Maine and southern New England, cutting a formerly straight coastline into the jagged array of bays, inlets, and harbors and forming the 4,613 islands off the coast of Maine.

15,000 years before present: Glacial landforms still evident in Maine, especially Down East, are created by the glacier's retreat.

13,000 to 11,500 years before present: Paleo-Indians, nomadic people who used fluted points to hunt big game, settle in Maine.

1000 AD: Norse sailors, led by Leif Erikson, arrive in Newfoundland and Nova Scotia. Although a Norse coin was found in Maine, and some believe the Vikings arrived here, others believe the coin was taken in trade.

1524: Giovanni da Verrazzano, an Italian explorer sailing for France, is identified as the first European to explore the coast of Maine.

1604: The first recorded European colony is established at the mouth of the St. Croix River in northern Maine by a French group led by

Pierre du Gua (or Guast) Sieur de Monts. A Huguenot nobleman, de Monts explored the New England coast with Samuel Champlain and helped him found Montreal.

1607: The first British colony, called Fort Saint George (also known as the Popham Colony), is established but fails to survive the first frigid winter. The town is now called Phippsburg.

1616-1619: Over 75 percent of Maine's Natives succumb to European diseases in "the Great Dying."

Fort Saint George

In 1607 (just months after the colony in Jamestown, Virginia) English settlers with the Virginia Company of Plymouth established Fort St. George at the mouth of the Kennebec River, ten miles south of what is now Bath, Maine.

The colony was led by George Popham, a nephew of the colony's chief backer and England's chief justice, who hoped to establish a center for trade in fur and timber, and, of course, the other draw of the new world, which was gold and silver.

In February 1608, George Popham died, and Raleigh Gilbert (nephew of Sir Walter Raleigh, a favorite of Queen Elizabeth I, but under her successor, James I, he was imprisoned and eventually put to death) succeeded him. There is some speculation that Gilbert lacked leadership skills, but also that first winter he learned of a huge inheritance, and this only accelerated the colony's demise.

The Maine winter also was brutal on the new colonists, and after only 14 months a decision was made to abandon it. In December half of the colonists returned to England. The other half stayed on and somehow or another managed to construct a small ship, a 30-ton pinnace they christened Virginia. After depositing the former colonists, the pinnace Virginia of Sagadahoc crossed the Atlantic again, ironically as part of a supply mission to Jamestown in 1609.

1622: The area is first called Maine by Sir Ferdinando Gorges, who along with John Mason is granted rights to lands that are now the states of Maine and New Hampshire. Although Gorges never set foot in the New World, his son, Robert, became Governor-General of New England from 1623 to 1624.

1634: Berwick becomes host to one of America's earliest sawmills, on the Salmon Falls River.

1640s: Maine is already shipping house frames and barrel staves to the Caribbean.

1652: Maine is annexed by Massachusetts because officials consider it a strategic first line of defense against the French and Indians.

1675-1763: Maine suffers several attacks by French and Indian forces during this period that starts with King Philip's War and ends with France giving up all its New World holdings to the English when the Seven Years War concludes.

1707: The John McIntire house is built in York; it remains one of the oldest still-standing structures today.

1735: A small paper mill is built on the Presumpscot River near what is now Portland.

1740: Maine's European-descended population hits the 12,000 mark.

1755: The Acadians are deported from Canadian Atlantic coastal communities to Maine and other New England locations because of their supposed loyalty to France.

TAKE5 MAINE STATE MUSEUM STAFF'S
LIST OF THE MUSEUM'S TOP FIVE EXHIBITS

The Maine State Museum in Augusta collects, preserves, and presents objects and specimens of Maine's natural sciences, pre-history, and history. Staff, many of whom have been caring for and interpreting the museum's collections for decades, selected the top five exhibits by looking at those that regularly delight visitors, represent the museum's diversity, and tell unique stories about Maine's past.

1. **The Lion**, an 1846 steam locomotive, dramatically greets visitors in the Maine State Museum's lobby. Made in Boston by Maine native Holmes Hinckley, the Lion is among the oldest surviving American-built railroad engines. It is exhibited with its tender, a car pulled behind that carried the water tank and firewood necessary to keep the steam engine running. The *Lion* worked for nearly 50 years as part of Washington County's Whitneyville and Machias Railroad. The 8-mile railroad line and its locomotives (the *Lion* and its twin, the *Tiger*) transported over 100 million board feet of sawn lumber from the mills of Whitneyville to schooners in Machiasport for shipment to markets nationwide.

2. **Paleo-Indian (Clovis Culture) Meat Cache:** Paleo-Indians were the first humans to live in Maine over 10,000 years ago. They originally built the meat cache, which consists of seven boulders set in a tight circle, in the Magalloway River Valley of western Maine. Caribou migrated through the valley by the tens of thousands. Paleo-Indians hunted them and stored the caribou meat in the center of the cache, under a pile of additional rocks to keep out scavenging animals. The meat cache may be the oldest surviving human-built structure in North America. Also on exhibit, fluted spear points excavated near the meat cache provide additional evidence of hunting activities of the Clovis Culture people in Maine.

3. **Peary Necklace:** Maine resident Robert E. Peary marked his wife Josephine's fiftieth birthday by giving her a beautiful tourmaline necklace. The year was 1913, just four years after Peary's discovery of the North Pole, one of his several Arctic expeditions that would not have been possible without Josephine's devoted support. Peary carefully planned the necklace to be made completely of Maine materials by

Maine people. The necklace's ten perfectly matched green tourmaline gemstones were mined at Auburn's Mt. Apatite and faceted by early Maine gemologist John S. Towne. A Portland jeweler made the necklace's chain and settings with gold panned from the Swift River near Byron.

4. **The 20th Maine Battle Flag and Captured Confederate Revolver** featured in the museum's Civil War flag exhibit inspires awe among museum visitors. Maine men died as they followed this flag in the fierce fighting on Little Round Top during the Battle of Gettysburg. Had the 20th Regiment Maine Infantry failed to hold the defensive line that day, the thinly stretched Union forces would likely have met defeat. His regiment out of ammunition, the 20th Maine's leader, Colonel Joshua Chamberlain, ordered a bayonet charge down the hill into the oncoming Confederate forces. Sword in hand, he led his men until confronted by a Confederate soldier wielding both a sword and a "big navy revolver." Chamberlain quickly captured his attacker. The pistol on exhibit is the one that Chamberlain described when he later wrote: "I passed him (the Confederate soldier) into the custody of a brave sergeant at my side, to whom I gave the sword as emblem of his authority, but kept the pistol with its loaded barrel, which I thought might come in handy soon, as indeed it did."

5. **The Spear Mill**, the literal and thematic centerpiece of the museum's "Made in Maine" exhibit, is a spectacular 3-story water-powered woodworking mill, complete with a running stream. The mill came to the museum collection from Warren, Maine. Its working turbine, shafts, belts, gears, and large wooden pulleys vividly demonstrate how, in the mid-1800s, water was moved, and its energy transformed, to operate machinery of all kinds. A long ramp in the exhibit gradually winds around the mill, enabling close-up views of the moving parts. On the ramp's opposite side, historical settings such as a sewing room, blacksmith shop, wool carding mill, and shops for making furniture, shoes, and bamboo fishing rods reveal stories of Maine people at work and the amazing variety of products they created.

The Maine Law

The world's first total abstinence society was founded in Portland in 1815. By 1834, temperance societies throughout Maine banded together in a statewide organization that quickly developed enough political clout to pass the first ban on the sale of alcoholic beverages.

One of the standard bearers of the movement was Portland mayor Neal S. Dow, a zealous reformer who became internationally recognized as the "Father of Prohibition." By 1851, Dow was powerful enough to get Maine Governor John Hubbard to sign off on a law that pushed Maine to become the first state in the union to pass a total ban on the manufacture and sale of liquor.

The so-called "Maine Law" became known across the country, and was one of the building blocks on the road to prohibition. (The Civil War only served to interrupt abstinence's march to a constitutional amendment in 1919.) Prohibition's detractors looking to bring Dow to his knees found it in one of the provisions of the "Maine Law."

Under the law, a judge was compelled to issue a search warrant if any three citizens accused a person of having alcohol. Word quickly spread that there was a cache of spirits in a Portland building being overseen by Dow. By evening time on June 2, 1851, upwards of 3,000 rioters were outside the building calling for Dow's head. (By this time, it didn't matter that the liquor was legal, and was intended for doctors and pharmacists.)

After it was clear that the police could not handle the crowds, Dow spooked and ordered in the militia. He gave orders to shoot to disperse the crowd. One man was killed and seven more were injured in what became known as the Portland Rum Riots. For his part Dow would be prosecuted (he was acquitted) under the provisions of the Maine Law. Although he would run politically again and again, his heavy-handed tactics all but derailed his political ambitions. In 1856, the Maine law was repealed.

1775: On June 12, the first naval battle of the American Revolution is fought off the coast of Machias. Called "The Lexington of the Seas," the battle saw the *Margaretta* captured and the British flag "struck" for the first time in the Americas.

1775: Benedict Arnold, one of the American Revolution's finest generals, leads a band of revolutionaries through Maine but fails to capture British holdings in Quebec City. Later Arnold is branded a traitor.

1783: Massachusetts, which includes Maine, abolishes slavery.

1785: Maine's first newspaper begins. *The Falmouth Gazette and Weekly Advertiser* is used to promote separation from Massachusetts.

1794: Bowdoin College becomes Maine's first post-secondary institution.

1800: A York novelist, Sally Wood, writes *Julia and the Illuminated Baron*, Maine's first novel on record.

1800: Maine's population reaches 150,000.

1800: The US government's oldest continuously-running naval shipyard opens at Kittery. The Portsmouth Naval Shipyard launches its first ship in 1815.

1820: Maine separates from Massachusetts and becomes a state on its own as part of the Missouri Compromise.

1832: Maine's state capital moves from Portland to Augusta.

1836: John Ruggles of Thomaston, Maine, is issued Patent #1 by the US Patent Office for his "Locomotive Steam Engine for Rail and Other

Roads." A lawyer elected to Congress in 1835, he helped reorganize the office and earned the title "Father of the Patent Office."

1839: Governor Fairfield makes Maine the first and only state ever to take military action against a foreign power when he send troops to deal with a boundary dispute between New Brunswick and northern Maine. No blood was shed, however, and the dispute was settled peacefully.

1842: The Webster-Ashburton Treaty of 1842, signed by US Secretary of State Daniel Webster and UK Privy Counselor Alexander Baring, settles the Maine/New Brunswick border when both territories agree to compromise.

1851: Harriet Beecher Stowe starts writing her legendary novel, *Uncle Tom's Cabin*, in Brunswick, inspiring those who would abolish slavery before the Civil War. An instant best-seller and translated into 23 languages, it is considered the most famous antislavery book. The Harriet Beecher Stowe House at 63 Federal Street, Brunswick, is a National Historic Landmark owned by Bowdoin College but is not open to the public.

1851: The so-called Maine Law is passed making Maine the first state in the union to ban the manufacture and sale of alcohol. Portland rum riots ensue.

1853: The Grand Trunk Railway is built to connect Maine with the St. Lawrence River in Montreal and the Canadian Maritimes. Portland is the winter port for Canadian trade.

1856: Maine Law is repealed.

1860: Hannibal Hamlin, a native of Paris, Maine, becomes Abraham Lincoln's vice president. The first Republican party vice president, he first served in the US Senate, the House of Representatives, two terms in the Maine legislature, and briefly as Maine governor.

1863: Brunswick native Joshua Chamberlain successfully defends Little Round Top against Confederate troops at the Battle of Gettysburg during the Civil War. Chamberlain's actions arguably served as the turning point of that battle.

1866: Fire destroys much of downtown Portland in the district now called the Old Port. Only two people die, but 1,800 buildings are reduced to ashes and 10,000 people are left homeless.

1888: Melville W. Fuller, a native of Augusta, Maine, and a Bowdoin College graduate, becomes the Chief Justice of the US Supreme Court.

1920s: South Paris enjoys a national reputation as "Toy Town," the country's largest concentration of producers of toys, including wooden sleds.

1931: Governor Percival Baxter, a native of Portland, Maine, begins buying land in northern Maine for the purpose of establishing a game reserve. Over the next 30 years, Baxter purchases more than 90,000 acres. This land is generously donated toward the establishment of Baxter State Park.

1936: Maine experiences disastrous spring flooding, resulting in $25 million in damages.

1947: Maine's most devastating forest fire destroys some 200,000 acres. More than 10,000 acres of this are in Acadia National Park. 851 homes and 397 cottages are lost.

1948: Skowhegan native and former Republican Congresswoman Margaret Chase Smith is elected to the US Senate, making her the first woman ever to be voted into this office, the first woman to serve in both

TAKE 5 FIVE MEMORABLE MAINE
STORIES DON CARRIGAN HAS COVERED

Don Carrigan is a reporter for WCSH-TV in Portland. He has been covering news in Maine since 1973, as a reporter, anchor and news director for WLBZ-TV in Bangor, and as executive producer of public affairs for Maine Public Broadcasting Network (MPBN). He also served for three years on the staff of US Senator Bill Cohen. He grew up in the town of South Bristol, graduated from Lincoln Academy and the University of Maine at Orono. After 35 years as a Maine reporter, here are five out of many moments that stand out.

1. **Fort Kent, May 1974:** We're shooting my first documentary, about the controversial Dickey-Lincoln Hydro Dam proposed. The night before, we'd been up way too late, being apparently the only two English speakers in a bar full of French Canadian woodsmen and locals. Needless to say, a great time. We're staying at Rock's Motel and Hot Dog Stand, the only motel in town. I had asked for a 5:30 wake-up call. But there are no phones in the rooms. At the appointed time, we're awakened by a fist pounding on the door and a woman's voice with a wonderful Franco accent shouting: "Hey, five-thirty! Time to get up!"

2. **Mars Hill Mountain, July 4, 1976:** It's America's Bicentennial, and Mars Hill is believed to be the first place in the US to see the sunrise that day. Maine's Second District Congressman, Bill Cohen, is the featured speaker for the event. The sunrise ceremony is beautiful, we get it all on film, and everyone heads back down the mountain. My photographer and I fly back to Bangor with Cohen in a small chartered plane, landing around 6 am. Cohen is all alone, and has no car, so we drop him off at his mother's house. As we drive away he's standing on the doorstep, ringing the bell or knocking. He evidently has no key. Something about that scene reminded me of a kid in high school, after a long night out with his pals, trying to get in without being noticed. Bill Cohen, of course, went on to become a prominent US Senator and then US Secretary of Defense.

3. **Sidewalks of Bangor, Spring 1975:** In 1975, Jimmy Carter was just laying the groundwork to win his party's nomination for president. He came to Bangor to meet with local Democrats. After covering the meeting, we were getting ready to leave when I spotted a man

standing alone on the sidewalk. It was Carter, waiting for someone to pick him up. I walked over to him and we talked for a few minutes, just the two of us, alone on that morning sidewalk in downtown Bangor. I don't think I really believed then he had any chance of becoming president of the United States. Eleven years later, I talked with Carter again in Bangor, on the day the space shuttle Challenger exploded. By chance, Carter was flying into Bangor on a charter flight from overseas. We stood on the airport stairs, alone again except for my photographer, talking about the tragedy.

4. **Lobstering with Lew Alley, July 2003:** Commercial fishermen are Maine's version of the old west cowboy: Independent, hard-working, willing to face some danger in what they do, and also great characters. Lobsterman Lew Alley was all those things. I had known Lew much of my life, and featured him in a story on lobstermen who are still working in their seventies and eighties. On the water, I saw an expert at work. I asked Lew about memorable days on the water. He told me about one day, years before, when he was hauling traps over towards Pemaquid Point. Suddenly, right in front of the boat, a killer whale came leaping out of the water. Lew described every piece of that scene. "Most beautiful thing I ever saw," he said. Now Lew might have been pulling my leg with that story — he liked doing that. But I hope not. I hope the story is true. I like the idea of that brief meeting, those two strong, beautiful, independent critters, looking at each other, both masters of the sea.

5. **The Millennium, Augusta, 11:59 pm, December 31, 1999:** The dreaded Y2K was finally here. We're in the "bunker," a basement room at the Maine Emergency Management Agency in Augusta, with about 70 other people to see if society is going to go haywire when the clocks strikes midnight. In this room are emergency officials (local, state, and federal), police, people from hospitals, power companies, and airports. All eyes are glued to computer screens that monitor their systems. The countdown comes and... nothing. We hit midnight, then 10 seconds past, then 30 seconds. Everything is still working. The room is silent. Y2K has hit, and there is no problem. We all look around at each other, until finally a quiet voice somewhere in the room says: "Well, Happy New Year."

houses of Congress, and the first Maine woman to serve in either house. She was also the first person to stand up to Senator Joseph McCarthy and his anti-Communist witch-hunt on the floor of the Senate. Her record still holds as the longest-serving woman in the Senate.

1955: The Maine Turnpike reaches Augusta.

1968: The University of Maine system is established, creating public post-secondary institutions in various parts of the state.

1974: James Longley is elected the first Independent governor of Maine, as well as the first Independent governor in the modern history of the two-party system in the United States.

1976: The last log drive in the US is held on the Kennebec River.

1979: Following a failed bid for the presidency, Rumford native and Democrat Senator Edmund Muskie replaces Cyrus Vance as President Jimmy Carter's Secretary of State.

1980: President Carter signs the Indian Land Claims agreement which ends disputed claims over the legality of treaties signed two centuries earlier, when Indians in Maine gave land to Massachusetts, and later Maine. The settlement gave the Penobscot Nation, the Passamaquoddy Tribe, and the Houlton Band of Maliseets $54.5 million to buy land that would be held in trust by the federal government.

1982: Ten-year-old schoolgirl Samantha Smith, of Manchester, Maine, writes to newly elected Soviet leader Yuri Andropov, asking if he plans to try to avoid nuclear war. He writes back, saying he wants to avoid war, and she becomes a media darling. A year later, she flies to the USSR with her parents to spend two weeks as a guest of the government. After the trip, she is called "America's Youngest Ambassador." She and her father are killed in a plane crash in Auburn, August 1985, and a foundation focusing on world peace is established in her name.

1984: Freeport native Joan Benoit Samuelson wins the gold medal in the first women's Olympic marathon event at the 1984 Summer Olympic Games in Los Angeles, California.

TAKE5 W. JAMES COOK'S FIVE
DOUBLE-EDGED CHANGES IN MAINE

Though born in Martinsville, Maine, James Cook lived for years in NYC where he worked for a musical lyrics company, working on Broadway shows with the likes of Carolyn Leigh, Cy Coleman, and Marvin Hamlisch. Cook is also a former lobster fisherman who realized there were easier ways to be poor.

1. Used to be I knew everyone who lived within fifteen miles of my house. It was a secure feeling. Nowadays there are a lot of people "from away" living in our small town and I don't even know half of my neighbors. That's bad. But they're interesting and worldly people, and when you do meet them you can talk about something other than lobster bait. That's good.

2. There are 32 houses on our little cove that weren't here in the good old days. That's bad for the pristine shoreline, but it's good that they all contribute to the tax base.

3. There are all manner of stores and restaurants that don't fit into Maine's Down East image. It erodes our "quaint character," but it sure makes living here easier and more rewarding.

4. The number of Maine "artists" has exploded and galleries have literally taken over some towns. That makes our economy less broadly based, but on the positive side it does give you something other than Wyeths to look at.

5. The people from away tend to drive ego cars and build very un-Maine houses, which makes the area seem more and more like New Jersey. But at least a big percentage of them new people are Democrats. And that is good.

1988: Waterville native Senator George J. Mitchell is elected US Senate Majority Leader. He won the Democratic nomination for governor in 1974 but was defeated in the general election by Independent James Longley.

1990: Great Northern Paper Company is acquired by the Georgia Pacific Corporation.

1994: Brunswick resident Angus King is elected governor, becoming only the second popularly elected Independent governor in the state and US.

1997: Bangor native, Senator William Cohen is sworn in as President Clinton's Secretary of Defense.

1998: Maine's worst natural disaster, the Ice Storm of '98, hits the state in the first week in January.

1998: Former Senator George Mitchell, appointed in 1995 as special envoy to Northern Ireland, is credited with negotiating the Belfast Peace Agreement, signed on Good Friday.

1999: Author Stephen King, walking on the shoulder of Route 5 near Lovell, is struck by a car and almost killed.

2000: Maine introduces a law banning all racist or derogatory place names.

2002: John E. Baldacci is elected Governor of Maine and reelected four years later.

2003: Great Northern Paper Company that once produced more than one-third of all US newsprint output declares bankruptcy after its modernization efforts fail in weak product markets.

2009: President Barack Obama appoints George Mitchell as Special Envoy to the Middle East on January 22.

2010: Lewiston singer-songwriter, Ray LaMontagne receives two Grammy nominations and wins the award for Best Contemporary Folk Album.

2011: Wealthy conservationist Roxanne Quimby proposes to donate 70,000 acres of remote land in northern Maine for the creation of a national park.

2011: Tea Party favorite Gov. Paul LePage's first year in office is backed by the first Republican-controlled Legislature since the 1960s.

2011: The "Redneck Olympics" were held in Hebron, Maine. Events included the wife-carrying competition, toilet seat horseshoes, the greased watermelon haul, bobbing for pigs feet, a mud run and tire popping.

2012: The first-in-the-nation tidal turbine began generating electricity and providing power to the grid from easternmost Maine's Cobscook Bay, in the Bay of Fundy near Lubec. The turbine can generate 180 kilowatts of electricity, enough to power 30 homes.

2014: The Bangor Police Department's humorous blog, called the "Duck of Justice," whose logo sports a small waterfowl with a badge, earns a national following.

2014: Controversial Tea Party governor LePage unexpectedly wins re-election in another three-way race.

2015: Best-selling novelist Stephen King, erroneously criticized by Gov. LePage for not paying his taxes, tweets "Governor Paul LePage implied that I don't pay my taxes. I do. Every cent. I think he needs to man up and apologize."

Maine Essentials

Origin of the Name: Attributed to Sir Ferdinando Gorges, it is possible Maine was named for a small village on the coast of England once named Maine, or Gorges' family lived near a village called Broadmayne, sometimes called Maine, Meine, or Parva Maen (Little Maine). In 2001, Maine established Franco-American Day, which said the state was named after the Old French province of Maienne, meaning "river of the middle." A prevailing theory, however, is nautical in origin. The "main" or "main land" distinguishes the bulk of the state from its numerous islands.

License Plate: Maine issued registration plates for cars in 1905. The first and only plate slogan, "Vacationland," appeared on the plate in 1936. A chickadee perched on a pine branch has illustrated the general issue plate since July 1, 1999. Prior to that date, a red lobster adorned the plate. There are also 22 specialty plates available to the general public for a fee to support various causes that range from the lobster industry to breast cancer research.

Motto: *Dirigo* ("I Lead")

Coat of Arms: A new but identical seal was ordered in 1880 after a Fusionist Secretary of State destroyed the original following an election loss. The Coat of Arms contains the original seal, designed in 1820, and is still in use today. It pictures "on dexter side, an Husbandman, resting on a scythe; on sinister side, a Seaman," a moose-deer, a mast-pine tree (a tall, straight pine good for making ships' masts), and in the foreground land and sea, the name of the state and the whole surrounded by a crest topped by the North Star. Oddly, there are no official colors for the seal or the Coat of Arms.

State Flag: Adopted in 1909, the flag has no official colors, but it is generally represented as a blue field with the Coat of Arms showing a green pine tree, green grass and a brown moose. Some examples, however, show purple trees behind the pine tree, or even yellow, pink, or red. The original Maine flag, in use from 1901 to 1909, was a simple pine tree with the North Star above.

Statehood: Maine became the 23rd state on March 15, 1820.

State Nickname: Pine Tree State

Tourism Slogan: Maine, The Way Life Should Be

State Tartan: The oldest state tartan in the US, designed in 1964 by Nova Scotian Sol Gillis, it has four colors: azure blue for the sky, royal blue for the waters, dark green for the forests, and a thin red line for the "bloodline" of Maine people.

Did you know. . .

. . . that in 2003 Maine was the first state in the nation to give portable, wireless personal computers to all seventh- and eighth- grade students and their teachers?

State Capital: Augusta

Largest City: Portland

Time Zone: Eastern Standard Time (or Eastern Daylight Time)

Civic Holidays: Maine celebrates all federal holidays and the April holiday it uniquely shares with Massachusetts, Patriot Day, which recognizes the battles of Lexington and Concord which launched the American Revolution. Federal holidays are New Year's Day, Martin Luther King, Jr. Day, Presidents Day, Memorial Day, Independence Day, Labor Day, Columbus Day, Veterans Day, Thanksgiving Day, and Christmas Day.

Location: In the northeastern corner of the United States, bordering the Atlantic Ocean to the east, the state of New Hampshire to the southwest, the Canadian provinces of New Brunswick to the northeast and Quebec to the northwest. Maine is the northernmost portion of New England and the easternmost state in the US.

Area Code: 207

System of Measurement: The United States Customary System (aka English, Imperial or standard units)

Voting Age: 18

Drinking Age: 21

Did you know. . .

. . . that Maine is the only state in the continental US to be bordered by only one other state?

TAKE5 CHRIS FAHY'S FIVE FAVORITE
NONFICTION BOOKS ABOUT MAINE

Christopher Fahy is a novelist and poet who has written about Maine for 40 years. He has written 16 books, including novels in the horror and suspense genres, and won the literary prize from the Maine Arts Commission for a book of short stories set in Maine. He is a writing instructor and helps organize the annual poetry festival at the University of Maine in Augusta, for which he was given a special award by the university. He also worked for 20 years as a counselor for the blind and visually impaired.

1. *The Coast of Maine* by **Louise Dickinson Rich:** A concise discussion of the geography, history, and development of the Maine coast, including islands, told in a brisk and breezy style. Includes some photographs, a number of entertaining stories (many of which are probably true), and a long list of things to see and do in various towns. Rich became famous for We Took to the Woods, her account of going back to the land long before it was fashionable. The woods she took to were also in Maine, and this is a book you should read if you want an in-depth description of one particular area of the state.

2. *Northern Farm* by **Henry Beston:** Beston describes a year in the life of his inland farm in the late 1940s; he delves into the history of his land, the changes of the seasons, his relationships with his neighbors, and patterns of work. His many astute observations of nature are told in a clear yet poetical prose. Each chapter contains a diary entry describing the events that are happening at the time he is writing. This provides a down to earth counterpoint to his philosophical and speculative notations.

3. *Summer Island* by Eliot Porter: Photographer Porter spent every summer since childhood on Great Spruce Head Island in Penobscot Bay. He captures the beauty of this and other islands in superb photographs, many in color, pairs them with quotes from poets and naturalists, and tells about his island's past and his discoveries while growing up there. Porter's eye is exquisite. Anyone who studies his photographs will make discoveries of their own, and anyone who carefully reads the text will have a better idea of what to look for while exploring Maine's woods and beaches.

4. *Night Train* at Wiscasset Station by Lew Dietz and Kosti Ruohomaa: In the 1940s and 50s, Ruohomaa took hundreds of photos of Maine people and places, many of which appeared in Life magazine. The best of these are included in this volume, which documents a way of life that was starting to disappear. Dietz provides essays on Maine's landscape, weather, and ways.

5. *Focused on the Coast* by Neal Parent: Excellent contemporary photos of, among other subjects, fishermen at sea, crisp shadows on snow, sailboats, waterfowl, and fog-shrouded harbors. Parent captures the rhythm and feel of what he photographs—an abandoned farm, a rocky shore during a storm—and puts the viewer right there. His gallery is located in downtown Belfast and every visitor to that city should be sure to stop by.

You Know You're From

- You can see Canada from your house.
- You call four inches of snow "a dusting."
- Your snow blower gets stuck on the roof.
- Your central heating system is fueled by large logs.
- More than half the meat in your freezer is moose.
- You call the area around your back door "the dooryard."
- You use "wicked" as a multipurpose part of speech.
- Your dog eats better than you do, and more often.
- You know a lobster pot is a trap, not a kettle.
- Your basement is called "downcellah."
- You buy your shrimp, berries, and Christmas wreaths from pickup trucks on the side of the road in season.
- You don't use your car's turn signal because everyone knows where you're going.
- You eat supper at night and dinner at noon.
- You know how to pronounce Calais, Damariscotta, Wytopitlock, and Saco.
- You eat ice cream with flavors like "Moose Tracks" and "Maine Black Bear."
- You know that "stove up" has nothing to do with cooking.
- Dressing up means wearing a tie with your flannel shirt.
- You've had a vacation from school just to help the family pick potatoes.
- The hardware store is busier on any Saturday than the toy stores are at Christmas.
- You leave your car running while you run into a store.
- Driving is better in the winter because the potholes get filled with snow.
- Your idea of a traffic jam is ten cars waiting to pass a tractor on the highway.
- You've had arguments over the comparative qualities of fried dough.
- You know the "Counties of our State" song.
- You can name all the seasons: Tourist, Foliage, Snowmobile, and Mud. (Or Winter and August.)
- "Vacation" means going to Bangor for the weekend.
- Your summer home is a "camp" less than half an hour from your house.
- You measure the distance between places in hours, not miles

Maine When . . .

- You've made meals out of a Jordan's red-dyed hot dog, a bag of Humpty Dumpty potato chips, and a can of Moxie soda.
- The local paper covers national and international headlines on one page but requires six pages for local sports.
- You often switch from "heat" to "A/C" in your car on the same day.
- You never say what you "paid" for an item but how much you "gave" for it.
- You know Bob Marley is a comedian, not a singer.
- You know 24/7 refers only to the hours at L.L. Bean.
- You go to the dump and bring back more than you took.
- You've watched *Murder She Wrote* and snickered at the stupid fake accents and the west coast boats shown in the intro.
- You brake for fiddleheads.
- You know how to find the rope swing at the quarry swimming hole.
- Your "luxury vehicle" is a 12-year-old pickup.
- The bumper jack in your pickup will lift a house.
- You've gone to a Grange bean supper.
- You design your kids' Halloween costumes to fit over a snowsuit.
- You have more miles on your snow blower than on your car.
- You install security lights on your house and garage and leave both unlocked.
- It takes you three hours to go to the store for one item even when you're in a rush because you have to stop and talk to everyone.
- You carry jumper cables in your car and your girlfriend knows how to use them.
- Your aunt, grandmother, cousins, second cousins, fifth uncle, etc., all live within ten miles of you.
- You know that the Maine Turnpike is for the tourists; real Mainers take the back roads.
- You wouldn't eat Manhattan clam chowder or beans in tomato sauce if you were starving!
- You use a down comforter in the summer.
- There's a vegetable stand within 10 minutes of your house.
- You garden with a full head net during black-fly season.
- Even your school cafeteria made good chowder.

Population: Maine has 16 counties, 22 cities and 424 towns with a total population of 1,317,207, a 1.5 percent increase since 2000. Between 1990 and 2000, the population increased by 3.8 percent. Projections say Maine residents will reach 1.4 million by 2025.

Population Density: Maine's land area covers 2,000 square miles with the average number of persons per mile estimated at 42.7.

TAKE5 BRET GILLIAM'S TOP FIVE
REASONS HE MOVED TO MAINE FROM THE CARIBBEAN

Bret Gilliam moved to Maine following 25 years in the Virgin Islands and the surrounding Caribbean. He is a widely published author, photographer and filmmaker who also specializes in legal consulting for diving and marine litigation.

1. You can actually go outside without melting from heat stroke from June to September.

2. None of those damned palm trees ever changed colors in the fall.

3. Weather: Snow is the epitome of peaceful tranquility, hurricanes blow you away. . . literally.

4. Drivers know which side of the road to drive on (most of the time).

5. Crime in Maine means someone's shed got robbed of a snow blower; in the Caribbean crime involves machetes, handguns, and voodoo.

How Maine Compares: Maine is the least densely populated of all the New England states. Vermont is ranked 30th in the US at 67.2 people per square mile, followed by New Hampshire in 20th place with 146.7. Connecticut is ranked fourth in the US with 722.9, while Massachusetts is third, with 822.7. Tiny Rhode Island beats its neighbors, second in population density in the US, at 1,012.3. The US average is 86.2. The District of Columbia (Washington, the nation's capital), while technically not a state, is first in density, with 9,581.3 people per square mile.

More Trees than People: Maine ranks 39th in size, but 40th in population in the US. More than half of Maine's population lives on only one-seventh of the land, within 25 miles of the sea. Nearly half the state is uninhabited. Ninety percent of the state is covered in trees. It's the most heavily forested of the states.

POPULATION BREAKDOWN

	Total	% of State Population
Male	641,623	48.8 percent
Female	673,157	51.2 percent

- Persons under 5 years old: 5.4 percent
- Persons under 18 years old: 21.3 percent
- Persons over 18 years old: 78.5 percent
- Persons 65 and older: 14.7 percent
- Median age: 41.1 years
- US average: 36.4 years

Did you know...

. . . that the Maine County Song is sung to the tune of "Yankee Doodle Dandy" in all Maine elementary schools as a way to teach students the names of Maine's 16 counties?

They said it

"Did you ever see a place that looked like it was built to enjoy? Well this whole state of Maine looks that way."

– Will Rogers, American humorist

RURAL VS URBAN
Rural: 548,506
Urban: 768,701

HOME AND FAMILY
• Average household size: 2.35, compared to 2.60 in the US
• Average family size: 2.84, compared to 3.19 in the US

POPULATION AND SIZE OF COUNTIES

County	Size	Population
Androscoggin	459 square miles	103,793
Aroostook	6,453 square miles	73,938
Cumberland	853 square miles	265,612
Franklin	1,789 square miles	29,467
Hancock	1,522 square miles	51,791
Kennebec	879 square miles	117,114
Knox	374 square miles	36,618
Lincoln	457 square miles	33,616
Oxford	2,023 square miles	54,755
Penobscot	3,258 square miles	144,919
Piscataquis	3,770 square miles	17,235
Sagadahoc	250 square miles	35,214
Somerset	3,633 square miles	50,888
Waldo	724 square miles	36,280
Washington	2,528 square miles	33,941
York	989 square miles	186,742

Source: Government of Maine.

Hard Shell

It is hard to imagine today, but what every Maine school child comes to learn is that not all that long ago lobster was considered a "poor man's food." When coastal school children brought lobster sandwiches to school every day, it was proof positive of their dire economic straits. And what children didn't bring to school, enterprising Maine fishermen simply ploughed back into the ground to use as fertilizer for their gardens.

All that has changed now, of course. The mighty lobster has ascended to the realm of luxury food. It now cavorts with caviar and foie de gras at the finest restaurants in Manhattan and Europe. Even among Mainers today, a lobster feed has taken on ritualistic rigor. Arguments ensue over proper cooking methods.

Part of the mythology of the lobster has been transferred to the fishermen who harvest them. There are currently 6,312 commercial lobster fishermen in the state of Maine and they, along with the people they employ, are often the backbone of coastal communities. For visitors and locals alike there is something primal and satisfying to see the lobster boats in pretty fishing villages and to eat a Maine lobster within view of its origins. The humble lobster has indeed become a tourist draw in its own right.

Lobster has not so quietly become the most visible and valuable seafood product in the state and is worth more than $250 million each year. Although fishermen have mostly switched from wooden to wire traps, harvesting methods have largely remained unchanged for 200 plus years. For Mainers and visitors, lobsters and lobster fishermen are one of very few unchanged links to the past, and therefore not only occupies a place in the palate of the nation, but also in the mind and heart.

POPULATIONS OF MAINE'S LARGEST CITIES

Portland's city population is 64,249, but the greater metropolitan area population is measured at 230,000, nearly one-quarter of Maine's population. Lewiston's population is 35,690 and is the second largest city in Maine on its own, but the population is nearly always linked with neighboring Auburn. The area is usually referred to as Lewiston-Auburn, or colloquially as L.A. The combined population is 106,815. Auburn alone has a population of 23,602, ranking it fifth among Maine cities.

TAKE 5 BILLY COOK'S FIVE WAYS
TO HELP YOU SURVIVE A VISIT TO MAINE

A native of midcoast Maine, and a Harvard graduate, Cook has written about Maine and elsewhere for more than 40 years. His family traces its roots back to the very earliest European communities along the Maine and Canadian coast. His recent short story, "A Good Connection" is included in the anthology *Sunday Miscellany*.

1. **Don't fake a Maine accent**. The entire cast of *Murder She Wrote* failed miserably, and most of us would have loved the chance to throttle any of them. Fair warning.

2. **Leave your city driving habits at home**. When you're down there, you might need heavy of foot, but we're just not used to having people whip out in front of us. We're also used to a bit more space around us, and tend to brake really hard very suddenly when you ride on our bumpers.

3. **If you come in June, bring bug repellent**. If you come in July or August, bring your own parking space.

4. **Don't ask us, "What do you DO all winter?"** Mostly we just sit and twiddle our thumbs waiting for you to come back and entertain us.

5. **We're called "Mainers" from early to mid-summer, and after you've all been here a couple months we become "Maineacs."** Don't take it personal.

They said it

"Nature was here something savage and awful, though beautiful. I looked with awe at the ground I trod on, to see what the Powers had made there, the form and fashion and material of their work. This was that Earth of which we have heard, made out of Chaos and Old Night."

– Henry David Thoreau, in the essay "Ktaadn"
(modern spelling: Katahdin) The Maine Woods, 1864

- Bangor: 31,473
- South Portland: 23,742
- Biddeford: 22,072
- Augusta: 18,626
- Saco: 18,230
- Westbrook: 16,108
- Waterville: 15,621

ETHNIC IDENTIFICATION

	Maine	US
Caucasian	95.5 percent	74.1 percent
African American	1.1 percent	12.4 percent
Hispanic or Latino	1.1 percent	14.7 percent
American Indian	0.5 percent	0.8 percent
Asian	0.9 percent	4.3 percent
Foreign-born	2.9 percent	11.1 percent

Source: US Census Data.

ANCESTRY

The top 10 countries identified as the country of origin of the families, or ancestry, of Maine residents who don't identify their families simply as being from America. Note that there are two kinds of French. If these were not separated, French would be the biggest nationality.

	Number	Percent
English	274,423	21.5
French (except Basque)	181,663	14.2
Irish	192,901	15.1
French Canadian	110,344	8.7
German	85,553	6.7
Scottish	61,226	4.8
Scotch-Irish	33,575	2.6
Polish	24,982	2.0
Swedish	21,342	1.7
Dutch	13,267	1.0

RELIGIOUS AFFILIATION

Most Mainers identify as Christian (82 percent), and most of those as various kinds of Protestants (56 percent). But as for identification with individual churches, of the Christians, the largest number is Catholic.

Baptist: 16 percent
Methodist: 9 percent
Pentecostal: 6 percent
Church of Christ: 3 percent
Lutheran: 3 percent
Other Protestant or general Protestant: 18 percent
Roman Catholic: 25 percent
Other Christian: 1 percent
Other Religions: 1 percent
Non-Religious: 17 percent

They said it

"To hell with all my worries
They are negligible at best.
I leave for Maine tomorrow
Where my soul can take a rest."

— **Anonymous, from the Bangor and Aroostook Railroad's**
tourist magazine *In The Maine Woods*, **published in 1934**

MATCHED
Marriage rate in Maine: 7.5 per 1,000
Marriage rate in the US: 7.3 per 1,000

DETACHED
Divorce rate in Maine: 4.3 per 1,000
Divorce rate in the US: 3.6 per 1,000

HATCHED (2008)
Births in Maine: 14,200
Births in the US: 4,278,899

DISPATCHED (2008)
Deaths in Maine: 12,443
Deaths in the US: 2,397,615

Source: US Bureau of Census.

MULTILINGUAL
The percentage of Maine residents who speak a language other than English at home is 7.6, compared to a national figure of 19.5. In Maine, the primary language spoken besides English is French, at an average of 5.28 percent, while in Louisiana, the average is 4.6 percent. More people in Maine speak French at home than any other state.

They said it

GETTIN' OLD

Maine's median age of 43.5 years is the highest in the nation, according to US Census Bureau statistics, compared to a US median of 36.8 in 2009. Maine has 411,540 people between the ages of 45 and 65, but only 301,124 people between ages 20 and 39. But by 2030, projections indicate the labor force will be 25,000 fewer, meaning a greater future need for medical and other services for the elderly supported by a smaller work force.

HIGH SCHOOL GRADUATES

High school graduates or higher total 88.8 percent of Maine's population, compared to a national average of 84 percent. However, residents with a bachelor's degree or higher, at 25.9 percent, fall a little behind the US figure of 27 percent.

SCHOOL DAYS

Maine's public elementary, middle, and high schools are funded by a combination of local property taxes and state and federal taxes. Many are regionalized into consolidated districts, so many students are bused to school in nearby towns. Maine also has a magnet public boarding school: The Maine School of Science and Math (grades 10-12) in Limestone, Aroostook County, with 105 students.

POST-SECONDARY INSTITUTIONS

Maine has 45 colleges and universities. Students can earn an associate degree at 22 of the schools, a bachelor's at 19, and a graduate degree at 10. Maine hosts 19 private colleges and universities, 10 public colleges and universities, eight community colleges, specialty schools such as a criminal justice academy, boatbuilding schools, Maine Maritime Academy, a law school, the environmentally-focused College of the Atlantic, Portland School of Art, Bangor Theological Seminary, and three world-renowned private liberal arts colleges: Bowdoin College in Brunswick, Bates College in Lewiston, and Colby College in Waterville.

UNIVERSITY OF MAINE SYSTEM

The University of Maine System has seven campuses of which Orono is the "flagship" campus. The system also includes seven community colleges and nine off-campus satellite centers throughout the state.

Total enrollment for 2008-2009 was 23,688, down 3 percent from the previous year. Its non-resident enrollment of 4,299 students was the second highest in UMS history, and included students from 48 states and 60 countries. In the Distance Education area, online web-based courses are up 19 percent. Law school enrollment increased by 5.9 percent.

Tuition for a full-time undergraduate ranges from $5,700 for an in-state student at one of the smaller campuses to $7,170 at the Orono campus. Out-of-state students can expect to pay from $14,310 to $20,580. A regional program offers a special tuition break for students from other New England states, ranging from $8,550 to $10,770.

Did you know. . .

. . . that the first chartered city in the US was in Maine? The coastal community of York was chartered in 1641.

UMAINE TOTAL ENROLLMENTS

University of Maine (main campus, Orono): 11,818
University of Maine at Augusta: 5,617
University of Maine at Farmington: 2,265
University of Maine at Fort Kent: 1,343
University of Maine at Machias: 1,259
University of Maine at Presque Isle: 1,652
University of Southern Maine: 10,820 (Maine Law School: 254)

SPORTS

Mainers particularly love high school and college basketball and the Black Bears, UMaine Orono's hockey team. The state's small population may account for the fact that semipro teams sometimes don't stick around long. The state currently has three. Earlier, Bangor lost its Can-Am League Lumberjacks minor league baseball team. However, Maine anticipates a semipro basketball team affiliated with the Boston Celtics to move to Portland in 2010.

The Portland Pirates are the American Hockey League affiliate of the Anaheim Ducks of California. They came along in 1993, soon after another team, the Maine Mariners, folded. Team colors are red, black, silver, and white. The logo sports a cartoon pirate with a hockey stick.

The Portland Sea Dogs are the American League minor league affiliate team for the Boston Red Sox. The 2009 season marked the team's

Did you know. . .

. . . that Maine is the most sparsely populated state east of the Mississippi River?

Did you know. . .

. . . that if the 45th degree line of latitude that separates Vermont from Quebec were continued eastward, nearly two-thirds of Maine would lie north of the line?

16th season in Portland. They made four straight playoff appearances between 2005 and 2008.

The minor league MAINEiacs hockey team arrived in Lewiston in 2003, where they play in the Androscoggin Bank Colisee for the Quebec Major Junior Hockey League – the only US-based QMJHL team. The team started in Canada and played from several towns under different names. In 2007, the MAINEiacs won the 2007 President's Cup. After winning the 2007 President's Cup, the team fell into disarray. Following a few failed relocation attempts, the owners approved the sale to the league itself, ending the franchise completely.

Weblinks

Maine Historical Society

http://www.mainehistory.org/

Find out more about Maine's history through this website; lots of reading on the MHS Museum, the Longfellow House, and the MHS Library.

Maine State Government, facts and history

http://www.maine.gov/portal/facts_history/

Facts, archives, personal accounts of the 'good old days,' genealogy resources, maps, statistics, and more.

Did you know. . .

. . . that Maine had the highest net gain of any state in New England of people over the age of 65 moving to the state to retire?

Did you know. . .

. . . that 16 percent of Maine residences are owned by out-of-state residents or by Maine residents for seasonal, recreational, or occasional use?

MaineSpeak

The language of Maine is colorful, and if the accent is thick enough, nearly incomprehensible to someone "from away," even another New Englander. Many words and expressions come from the state's two primary historic occupations—woods work and seafaring.

These two occupations—still the two most dangerous in the country—not only contributed many words to the Maine lexicon, but probably gave rise to the laconic, economical, understated manner of speaking (way more adjectives than befits a Mainer).

The primary Maine accent derives from the English, Irish, and Scottish origins of the settlers, except in the St. John Valley, where French dominates. Many of the place names still bear their Native American origins, but are probably not pronounced anywhere near the original. Many French Canadians also migrated to work in the mills of cities such as Augusta, Waterville, and Lewiston, where a Maine French accent can still be heard.

If you're visiting Maine's third-largest city, Bangor, don't call it Banger (as Roger Miller did in "King of the Road") but BAN-gore. Saco is Socko, Damariscotta is DamURscotta and Calais is CAHLus.

The Airline: The 98-mile stretch of Route 9 between Bangor and Calais. A wild and woolly ride with spectacular hilltop views making the driver feel on top of the world. Fabulous in summer and fall, a bit hairy in winter. In recent years, the state shaved off some of the hills and straightened a few of the more harrowing curves. It took some of the risk (and fun) out of the ride, but it's still spectacular and still risky in bad weather.

Alewives: A fish in the herring family that swims up some Maine rivers to spawn.

All hands and the cook: Everyone.

A piece: An undetermined distance, as in, 'He lives down the road a piece.'

Art square: Flower-patterned rug in the parlor.

Ayuh: Yes (accent on the long A).

Back: To address; to back a letter before mailing it.

Backing and filling: A term from sailing. It means it looks like you're not making much headway, but you are.

Barrens: As in "blueberry barrens," fields where wild blueberries grow.

Beamy: Wide (as in a boat or a person).

Beans: Shorthand for the traditional Saturday night meal which always includes baked beans, and an indicator of ignorance, as in, "He don't know beans."

Blowdown: A forest area leveled by wind.

Blowing like stink: The same as blowing a gale – very windy.

Camp: A vacation house (small or large) usually on fresh water and/ or in the woods. Often not too far from the main house. Mainers don't see the need to go far from home for vacations. After all, they live in Vacationland.

Chance: Serendipity or luck (as in, "Open by appointment or by chance,") also, a ticket for a prize drawing, as in, "Do you want to buy a chance?"

Chicken dressing: Chicken manure, politely!

Chowder: Pronounced "chowdah," a soup made with lobster, clams, fish, corn or any combination thereof. Always milk-based, NEVER with a tomato base or it isn't chowder in Maine. Also a verb; making a noise as in, "The house chowdered all night."

Clambake: A party or gathering that may become noisy, as in, "The town meeting will be a real clambake this year."

Come into the wind: Wait a minute.

Cottage: A vacation house usually on salt water. Some of the "cottages" of wealthier families who spend summers here are mansions, but a typical Maine cottage is really a cottage.

The County: Aroostook County in northernmost Maine. The largest county east of the Mississippi River, its 6,829 square miles make it larger than Connecticut and Rhode Island combined, but fewer than 79,000 people live there. Best-known for the potato, it is also fast becoming a center for wind power.

Culch: "Stuff," the contents of attics, basements, and some flea markets.

Cull: A discount lobster, usually minus a claw, therefore lower in price.

Cunnin': The Maine word for cute.

Dinner: Pronounced "dinnah," the noon meal.

Dinner pail: Lunch box.

Dite: A very small amount.

Dooryard: The place outside the side door of the house; could be the yard or the driveway. The boat might be in the dooryard.

Down East: With the prevailing wind, the old coastal sailing route from Boston to Nova Scotia.

TAKE5 BETSY SHOLL'S FIVE PHRASES
THAT DEFINE MAINE

Betsy Sholl's seventh book is *Rough Cradle* (Alice James Books, 2009). She lives in Portland and teaches at the University of Southern Maine and in the MFA Program of Vermont College of Fine Arts. She was named Poet Laureate of Maine in 2006.

1. **Fir-fringed cold**
2. **Ghost oceans of fog**
3. **The country's jagged edge**
4. **Wharf light**
5. **Woods full of thrushes**

Downceller: In the basement (pronounced downCELLah).

Downstate: The rest of Maine, according to residents of the County.

Dry-ki: Driftwood, usually remnants of the logging industry.

Elegant: Often the Mainer's answer to the question, "How are you?"

TAKE5 FIVE MAINE EXPRESSIONS
FROM LUTHERA DAWSON

Luthera Dawson heard them all over her 100 years, and she wrote them down in her three books. She contributed heavily to the list of Maine terms in this chapter. MaineSpeak, as she called it, is part of a chapter she wrote for an anthology called "Salt and Pines." Born in Cushing on June 6, 1911, Luthera's first book, *Saltwater Farm*, is about growing up there. Beside the St. Georges continues the theme (including recipes!), and *Life Begins at 1440* recounts her sojourn in Washington, DC where she worked for the Internal Revenue Service during World War II. She now lived and wrote in Cushing, where she was keeper of Maine's unique language until her death in 2011.

1. **Don't give me that who struck John:** Don't start an argument.

2. **Two lights burning and no ship at sea:** Said of someone who is unnecessarily wasteful.

3. **When it looks like rain and don't, 'twun't:** All signs fail in a bad time.

4. **'Tis as 'tis and can't be no 'tiser:** Things can't be changed from their present (and probably bad) condition.

5. **Cold as a dog and the wind northeast:** That's pretty cold!

Exercised: Upset, angry. As in, "He was really exercised when Bert took his dinner pail."

Finest kind: Top quality, good news; an expression of general approval, also, a term of appreciation. Used to describe something or simply as an expletive.

TAKE5 FIVE MAINE WORDS
FROM JOHN GOULD

John Gould was a Maine author. These expressions are gleaned from his *Maine Lingo: Boiled Owls, Billdads, & Wazzats* book from 1975.

1. **Boiled owl:** A presumptive, last-ditch meal that in Maine cookery means there is nothing tougher.

2. **Billdad:** One of the mythical animals of the Maine woods, said to secure its food by standing on a bank and slapping trout with its tail. The noise, very like a beaver's warning slap, is a "wazzat," from the sport's usual query, "what's-at?" The billdad is small, about ankle high. Anyone scouting billdads is looking for a drink; if he finds one, he's had one.

3. **Clear gravy:** Extra profit, or an unexpected bonus. Gravy as an embellishment is standard ("gravy train") but adding clear seems a Maine-ism.

4. **Lay away:** Kindly term for destroying an animal: "We had to lay old Tige away."

5. **Witch:** Witch remains the favored Maine word for a water dowser, and it is applied to both men and women who divine underground water. Usually Mainers say in full, water-witch, and the divining is called 'water-witchin.' Although Mainers have about the same percentage of belief and disbelief as other people, there has never been any black-magic nuance in this use of witch.

Flat-ass calm: That mirror glassiness that you see on the ocean in early evening, dawn, or before a storm.

Flatlander: A person not from Maine.

Flowage: A water body created by damming, usually beaver handiwork.

Frappe: A thick drink containing milk, ice cream, and flavored syrup—as opposed to a milkshake, which does not include ice cream (but beware; a frappe offered in other parts of the United States is an ice-cream sundae topped with whipped cream!).

From away: Not native to Maine. People are "from away" for life, even if they moved to Maine as an infant. In the old days, it might even refer to someone who came from another Maine town.

Galamander: A wheeled contraption formerly used to transport quarry granite to building sites or to boats for onward shipment.

Gore: A sliver of land left over from inaccurate boundary surveys; Maine has Misery Gore, Coburn Gore, Hibbets Gore, and more.

Got done: Quit a job, or was let go. As in, "He got done at the lumber yard."

Harbormaster: Local official who monitors water traffic and assigns moorings.

Hardshell: A lobster that hasn't molted yet.

Jeezly: An adjective that means not so good; as in, "I've never seen such jeezly fishing."

Jizzicked: Done for, broken beyond repair.

Lobster car: A large floating wooden crate for storing lobsters – it keeps them in the water and alive.

TAKE 5 FIVE UNUSUAL MAINE
ATTRACTIONS

Most states have some unusual roadside attractions and Maine is no exception. We've listed here five of the biggest in size and some of the unusual in form.

1. **World's Largest Rotating Globe:** Appropriately named Eartha, this giant globe is visible from the highway and can be seen close-up inside the DeLorme Mapping Company in Freeport. Representatives of the Guinness Book of World Records made it official when they measured Eartha at just under 131 feet around and a tad over 41 feet across the middle, beating out a 33-foot rotating globe in Italy. Construction was completed in 1998. Tilted as is the earth on a 23.5 degree axis, Eartha is located in a three-story glass atrium of DeLorme headquarters in Freeport. CEO David DeLorme designed the globe which can be viewed from three observation levels – generally the South Pole, the Equator, and Greenland. It takes 18 minutes to complete its full rotation.

2. **14-Foot Crank Telephone:** The town of Bryant Pond is home to a 3,000 pound, 14-foot-tall black candlestick telephone, noting the town's distinction of being the last in the country to use hand-cranked telephones. The residents of Bryant Pond liked the hand-cranked phones, which were operated from a switchboard in the living room of the home of the phone company owners. In 1983, the old candlesticks were finally replaced by dial service. The huge metal sculpture by Maine artist Gil Whitman was unveiled and dedicated 25 years later to commemorate the Bryant Pond Telephone Company. Just before the phone system was finally upgraded, Bryant Pond residents tried to prevent modernization and adopted a slogan, "Don't yank the crank!"

3. **World's Tallest Indian:** The town of Skowhegan boasts the world's tallest Indian, which stands on a 20-foot high base and is 62 feet tall. This Native American was created by the late Cushing sculptor Bernard Langlais to commemorate Maine's 150th anniversary and is dedicated to Maine's Abenaki Indians. The sign at the statue's base reads: "Dedicated to the Maine Indians, the first people to use these lands in peaceful ways."

4. **31-Foot Paul Bunyan Statue:** Bangor, Maine and Akeley, Minnesota compete for the birth claim of fabled woodsman Paul Bunyan. Mainers believe he was born here on February 12, 1934. Bangor's 31-foot tall statue of a lumberjack weighs 3,700 pounds, not including the giant double-sided ax and pike he has in his hands. The statue was donated to Bangor in 1959 in celebration of the city's 125th anniversary and contains a time capsule to be opened in 2084. Maine's famous author, Stephen King, brought it celebrity in his 1986 novel, *IT*.

5. **Oldest Halfway to Equator Marker:** In 1896, a chunk of pink granite was placed in the eastern Maine town of Perry marking the 45th Parallel, halfway from the equator to the North Pole. Maine was the first state to recognize that site and since that time many other states lined up on the 45th Parallel have followed the town of Perry's lead with historical markers pointing out the distinction.

Low dreen tide: A very low tide.

Maine Guide: A person licensed to lead hunting and fishing trips in Maine.

Middlin' smart, thank you: The response when asked, "How are you?"

Mud season: Mid-March to mid-April when back roads and unpaved driveways become virtual tank traps. Sometimes Mainers will say they have winter, mud season, and August, but that's of course an exaggeration. Well, some years.

Mug up: Snack between meals or a coffee break.

Nasty neat: Extremely meticulous.

Near: Stingy.

Notional: Stubborn, determined; used to describe a person.

Pot: Trap, as in "lobster pot."

Rake: Hand tool used for harvesting blueberries.

Right out sideways: Very, very busy.

Right out straight: Busy.

Rusticator: A summer visitor, usually one who stays for the entire summer. A term that originated in the late 19th century when city families would come to the country – usually the coast or a big lake – and "rusticate" for the summer.

Sandpaper the anchor: Children underfoot, so grandmothers would find them some useless work to do to get them out of the way.

Scooch: To move sideways. As in, "Scooch over, will ya?"

Scrimey: "He's a scrimey bahstud" means he's a penny pinching miserly tightwad who couldn't bring himself to throw away his shaved whiskers.

Sea smoke: Heavy mist rising off the water when the air temperature suddenly becomes much colder than the ocean temperature.

Selectmen: The elected men and women who handle local affairs in small communities.

Shedder: A lobster with a new (soft) shell.

Shire town: County seat.

Shore dinner: The works; chowder, clams, lobster, and sometimes corn on the cob, too. The best ones are cooked underground on hot rocks using seaweed to create the steam that cooks the clams, lobster, and corn (not the chowder!) and eaten outdoors by the sea.

Short: A small, illegal-size lobster.

Slaruppy: Untidy, messy, or not feeling well.

Slumgullion: American chop suey (macaroni, ground beef, and tomato).

Smur: A foggy, dark haze on the horizon.

Snow in the woodbox: Pretty bad off; no wood, only snow to burn.

Some: Very (as in "It's some hot"). Used throughout Maine in every possible context.

Southerly smeach: Storm from the south.

Did you know. . .

. . . that the sign outside Hussey's General Store in Windsor reads: Guns, Wedding Gowns, Cold Beer? Draw your own conclusions.

Spleeny: Overly sensitive. It also means "having a low tolerance for pain."

Sternman: A lobsterman's helper (male or female) who does most of the pot hauling.

Supper: Pronounced "suppah," it is the evening meal eaten by Mainers around 5 or 6 pm (as opposed to flatlanders and summer people who eat dinner between 7 and 9 pm).

Tad: Slightly, a little bit.

Thank you, Ma'am: When you're riding large rollers and the boat crests the wave and suddenly drops out from under you into the trough, your stomach lurches and your heart leaps into your mouth...that's a "Thank you, Ma'am." Harty Cook from Jonesboro pronounced it "Thank you, Marm."

Thick-o'-fog: Zero-visibility fog.

Tomalley: A lobster's green insides, considered a delicacy by some, gross and disgusting by others!

Town landing: Public docking for boats, usually including a launching ramp.

Turn out (coastal version) / roll out (woods version): Rise and shine!

Under full sail: A well-endowed female.

Upattic: In the attic.

Whatevah: A more modern catch-all word that expresses a dite of disdain for the topic, or boredom with it, or a reluctant acceptance of an unwelcome fact.

Whoopie pie: The trademarked name for a chocolate cake-like snack that traditionally has a sweet, creamy, white filling, although a resurgence in popularity means it now comes in many flavors including pumpkin, maple, and blueberry.

Wicked cold: Frigid.

Wicked good: Excellent.

Williwaws: Uncomfortable feeling; people get the williwaws.

Wizzled: Wrinkled like a prune.

TAKE5 KENDALL MORSE'S FIVE DOWN EAST WORDS

Kendall Morse grew up in Machias, where he grew up with words seldom, if ever, heard in other parts of Maine. He's a Maine humorist, a folk singer with four recordings to his credit, as well as a Grammy nomination for "Singing Through the Hard Times," a double CD of songs written by his late friend Bruce "Utah" Phillips and sung by several top artists.

1. **Dido.** As in to "Cut up a dido" A bit of mischief, an act that could get you arrested. Originally, a Dido was a dance.

2. **Adam's off ox.** As in "I didn't know him from Adam's off ox." A stranger. The off ox was the one opposite the driver. The nigh ox was the one nearest the driver. If the driver was seated on the left side of the wagon the off ox would be the one on the right.

3. **Rackaboobob.** A mythical wild creature sort of like Ruth Moore's "Hangdowns".

4. **Savagrus.** Tough conditions, such as a hard winter or very foul weather.

5. **Hogag.** An undesirable person, a liar or a thief.

Place Names

Many of Maine's place names derive from the original names given to them by Native Americans, although the influence of French, English, and Irish settlers is obvious. There are some biblical names and a host of post-Revolutionary names, and a grouping of names that are dupes of those in Massachusetts that were named by settlers from those MA towns.

Some are fun to say, like Mooselookmegunitic. Others look simple, but are usually pronounced incorrectly by outsiders, for instance Bangor and Saco. You can travel the world, from China to Norway, and stay in Maine. Or you can seek Liberty, enjoy Freedom or hunt up a ghost on a landing.

Acadia: A Mi'kmaq term meaning "the earth/land," as in Acadia National Park. Originally named Sieur de Monts National Monument to honor the first explorer in 1604, Samuel Champlain, and the French Jesuits who worked with the natives at Iles des Mont Desert until the English destroyed the mission. The 47,000-acre park was renamed in 1929.

Allagash River (and town): An Abnaki term meaning "bark shelter." The Allagash Wilderness Waterway is a 92-mile stretch of unspoiled scenery in Aroostook County popular with canoers and rafters. The town of Allagash is an Irish-Scotch enclave in the mainly French St. John Valley.

Androscoggin River: An Abnaki term meaning "place where fish are dried/cured." Still a popular fishing place, the Androscoggin drops an average of eight feet per mile along its 178-mile course so it's always been important for manufacturing. Its flow powered sawmills, paper mills, and textile mills, which also meant it became severely polluted and helped instigate the Clean Water Act. Much cleaner now, a 14-mile stretch of the river still requires oxygen bubblers to keep fish alive.

Annabessacook: A lake in Monmouth whose name means "smooth water at outlet."

Aroostook: A Mi'kmaq term meaning "beautiful river." The name of the state's largest – bigger than Connecticut and Delaware combined – and northernmost county, is called simply "the County" by its residents. An inland farming region, Aroostook is best known for its potato farms.

Augusta: Maine's capital city was first explored by English settlers in 1607 by the short-lived Popham Colony, and later settled by the Plymouth Colony in the late 1620s. It was designated as the state capital in 1827.

Bailey's Mistake: This small village in the downeast town of Cutler can trace its name back to the poor navigation of a young sea captain. One night back in 1830, Captain Bailey was piloting a four-masted schooner, packed with cargo bound for Lubec, up the coast from Boston. The fog was thick, as it often is in those parts. Young Bailey mistook a dead end cove for the Lubec Narrows, which leads to that town's port. The ship grounded on what is now called Bailey's Ledge, where it remained until morning. Legend has it that the captain and crew were reluctant to return to Boston and confess their mistake to their bosses. Instead, they decided to unload the lumber they had been transporting and build homes on the spot, creating the village that is now known as Bailey's Mistake.

Benedicta: Bishop Benedict Fenwick, second Bishop of Boston, acquired the property deep in Aroostook County in 1834, planning to build a Catholic school. He wanted to populate the area first to have a community around the college, so he gave land to poor Irish immigrants arriving in Boston who promised to homestead. The Irish moved there, built St. Benedict's Catholic Church, took up farming, but Fenwick ended up establishing Holy Cross College in Worcester, MA. Benedicta was deorganized as a town in 1987 and is now governed as an unorganized territory with 225 residents.

Cadillac Mountain: Plenty of General Motors' Cadillac automobiles have made the drive to the 1,532-foot summit of Cadillac Mountain, the first location in the United States to see the sun each morning. Both car and peak are named for French explorer Antoine Laumet de La Mothe, Sieur de Cadillac. The French Crown granted the explorer much of Mount Desert Island in 1681. La Mothe later founded a colony in what was to become Detroit, home of American automobile industry, including GM.

Calais: Named for the French city but pronounced CAHL-us by Mainers, rather than Cal-AY.

Calendar Islands: The Chief Engineer for the British crown who surveyed Casco Bay in 1700 wrote that the bay had "as many islands as there are days in the year." In fact, there are 138 islands in the bay, give or take a few, not counting ledges that are often underwater. Nonetheless, Colonel W. Romer's assertion gave a nickname to the bay that stretches from Portland to Phippsburg. The bay's official name comes courtesy of Spanish explorer Estevan Gomez who noticed in 1525 that the bay is shaped like a helmet, or in Spanish, uno casco.

Cathance: The name means "the principal branch of a river." Pronounced "cat-hance," it refers to a river flowing through Topsham and Bowdoinham to Merrymeeting Bay, and to a stream in Dennysville.

Chebeague Island: An Abnaki term meaning "separated place." Pronounced Sheh-BEEg. In Casco Bay, Chebeague has a year-round population.

Chemquasabamticook Lake: An Abnaki term meaning "where there is a large lake and a river."

You Can Get There from Here

Maine has seven towns named for countries: Denmark, Sweden, Norway, Mexico, Peru, China, and Poland. Five of these are situated near each other in Oxford County, but China is located in Kennebec County and Poland is in Androscoggin County. Another town is named for part of a country: Wales, located in Androscoggin County.

Lore has it that many Maine towns were named in the late 1700s and early 1800s when people in many other countries were fighting for their freedom, which appealed to the independent Mainers.

Maine also has five towns named for cities in Italy: Rome, Verona, Sorrento, Palermo and Naples.

Often, towns are named by settlers pining for their former homes, but no Italians were numbered among the original residents of these towns. It is believed the townspeople simply admired the cities from afar. Go figure.

Five other towns are named for cities in five countries: Madrid, Vienna, Stockholm, Moscow, and Lisbon. Pronounce three of them in the conventional style, but if you want to sound like a Mainer, it's Ma-DRID and VYE-enna.

Nine of the foreign-named towns are honored by a signpost at the junction of Routes 35 and 5 at Lynchville. Erected in 1930, it is little surprise that the signpost often disappears.

Cobscook Bay: A Maliseet term meaning "rocks under water."

Cobbosseecontee Lake: An Abnaki term meaning "many sturgeon." Specifically, it was the place on the Kennebec River where the Indians fished for sturgeon. The nearby lake and stream may have been named for this area in the river.

Crotch Island: The smooth-grained granite quarried from the Maine coast has gone into monuments, capital buildings and other landmarks all over the east. Today the once-thriving quarries are mostly closed, but a few, including one on Crotch Island off the coast of Deer Isle, continue to operate. Crotch Island gets its name from the enormous trench that quarriers have carved out of its side over the years.

Damariscotta: An Abnaki term meaning "many alewives" pronounced Dam-UR-scotta by Mainers and regularly mispronounced by visitors and TV reporters.

TAKE5 FORMER NAMES

1. **Bar Harbor** used to be called Ahbaysauk; "place where clams are baked/dried." Also formerly called Eden.

2. **Lewiston Falls** used to be called Amitgon pontook; "place at the falls where fish are dried/cured."

3. **Portland** used to be called Machegony; "shaped like a large knee."

4. **Casco Bay** used to be called Aucocisco, source uncertain, but probably Maliseet or Mi'kmaq for "the head of the bay" and "mud." Or Abenaki for "heron.

5. **Augusta** used to be called Cushnoc; "head of tide."

Queen of the East

Although originally called Condeskeag Plantation by its 1769 British founders, Bangor came by its new name largely as a result of a renegade reverend. Legend has it that in 1791 settlers sent Rev. Seth Noble to Boston (Maine was then still part of Massachusetts) to incorporate the city and change its name to Sunbury. For some reason Noble changed his mind and named the city for his favorite Irish hymn.

Although Bangor today is the major cultural center for eastern and northern Maine, Bangor earned its early reputation as a rough and tumble town where lumberjacks and sailors kicked up their heels in "the Devil's Half-Acre," while the swells partied in their mansions. To commemorate the era, a statue of the mythical lumberjack, Paul Bunyan, graces the entrance to the downtown civic center.

Nicknamed "Queen City of the East" in the 19th century for its beautiful downtown, shade trees, and the elaborate Greek Revival and Victorian homes built by lumber barons, Bangor quite proudly and rightly called itself the "lumber capital of the world." When Portland and Maine went "dry" in 1851, Bangor managed to remain "wet," using the Bangor Plan, a system of institutionalized bribes. Flying in the face of the Maine Law of prohibition, Bangor boasted some 142 saloons downtown in 1890. The Great Fire of 1911 destroyed the city, but citizens rebuilt and Bangor continued to prosper. Downtown spiraled into decline in the '60s, but a revival started in the 1990s with waterfront beautification and an influx of small businesses—galleries, bookstores, and restaurants. Bangor also hosts the state's only casino and a riverside international folk festival in summer.

The third most populous city in Maine, Bangor is home to just over 31,000 residents, while the greater metropolitan area has a little more than 148,000. The most famous Bangor resident is international best-selling novelist, Stephen King. Since most of his voluminous output is in the horror genre, it's appropriate that King and family occupy a Victorian home surrounded by an iron fence topped with little bats.

TAKE**5** FIVE NAMES
LACKING IN IMAGINATION

1. **Ninemile Brook**
2. **Nineteen Mountain**
3. **Number Nine Mountain**
4. **Number One Brook**
5. **Number Seven Ridge**

Desert of Maine: Yes, there is a desert in Maine – or at least something that looks like one. The phenomenon can be traced back to the last ice age, when glaciers dropped massive deposits of sand across interior Maine. At this site, in Freeport, the shallow topsoil was eroded away, leaving a vast field of sand that has become a rather odd tourist destination.

Eggemoggin Reach: The eastern channel of Penobscot Bay. The name means "fish weir place."

Ghost Landing Bar: A spot in Allagash, Aroostook County, named for a logger killed by a falling pine. The core was rotten so it was left on shore. People claim his ghost asks passersby to roll the log into the water.

Grindstone: A place where river drivers sharpened their axes, an unincorporated settlement in Penobscot County, not surprisingly settled by people involved in the forest products industry.

Hell's Half Acre: This island is a bit larger than a half acre and its cobble beaches and panoramic views are far too pleasant to be associated with hell—but it is just south of Devil Island. No one knows for sure how either island got their names.

TAKE5 FIVE MUNICIPAL DESIGNATIONS
THAT ARE NOT CITIES OR TOWNS

1. **Minor Civil Division** is the designation of civil divisions of the state below the county level. Often abbreviated MCD, it includes townships which have no organized local governments, and organized local governments which are plantations, towns, and cities. Most MCD's are six mile squares, especially those in the later-settled northern two-thirds of the state.

2. **Plantations** are a type of minor civil division falling between township (or unorganized territory) and town. The term, as used in this sense in modern times, appears to be exclusive to Maine. A plantation is essentially a previously unorganized township that the state legislature has granted a limited form of self-government that is similar to, but simpler than, a town. Plantations are typically found in sparsely populated areas.

3. **Shire town**, also known as "county seat" or seat of government including the county offices of its Superior Court, sheriff, Registry of Deeds, Probate Court, and Register of Probate.

4. **Unorganized territory** represents a region of land, generally with less self-governmental powers than other regions, controlled by a specific government. Unorganized territories occur in 10 states. Maine has 36 territories contained in 14,052.47 sq. miles or 45.5 percent of the land area.

5. **Village corporation** is a form of local government creating a virtual "town within a town." They were especially popular in areas where "summer colonies" of non-residents preferred to operate their own administrative affairs separate from the parent town, often taxing themselves for fire, police, and other services beyond what the town would have provided. Most have been absorbed by the parent towns or have been incorporated as separate towns.

Junk of Pork Island: This island consists of nothing more than a rock formation sticking out of the water on the perimeter of Casco Bay. Some folks think it looks like a slab of pork. It also happens to be the only place in Maine where storm petrels come ashore to nest.

Katahdin: An Abnaki term meaning "the principal mountain." Maine's tallest mountain, Mount Katahdin, is located in Baxter State Park.

Malaga: "Cedar." Two Malaga Islands are associated with Maine; one in Phippsburg, one at the Isles of Shoals. The one off Phippsburg represents a shameful event in Maine history. In 1847, Malaga was settled by a freed slave who had saved his owner's life. His family was joined by others, constituting a mixed race of Irish, Scottish, Portuguese, and African-Americans. Mainlanders called the Malagaite residents an "eyesore" and a "maroon" society. In 1911, the governor forced residents off the island. Seven were committed to the Maine School for the Feeble Minded. Malaga was one of 274 Maine communities with a tiny number of black citizens.

Mars Hill: Mars Hill is a town in Aroostook County with a population of about 1,500 people. A British Army Chaplain held a service on a nearby mountain in 1790, and named the peak Mars Hill after a hill in Athens, where the apostle Paul was said to have taught the Athenians of his God. The town was later named after the mountain, which is now scattered with energy-producing wind turbines.

Massacre Pond: On a fall afternoon in 1703, Captain Richard Hunnewell of the British Army and twenty of his men wandered to this pond along the sandy shores of what is now Scarborough Beach. A party of more than 100 Indians ambushed the unarmed men, slaughtering Hunnewell and 18 others.

Matinicus Island: An Abnaki term meaning "far-out island." The year-round population of Matinicus in Penobscot Bay relies mostly on lobstering.

McGargle Rocks: This area was named for a river driver who was killed trying to clear a log jam. It is about a half mile below Big Brook campsites in Aroostook County, and the peak of the summit is 712 feet.

Meddybemps: One of several place names that translates "plenty of alewives." And it's cute and fun to say.

Portland

Portland is Maine's largest city, and its cultural, business, financial, retail, and culinary capital. The city's oldest parts are wrapped around Portland Harbor, bracketed by the two hills of the Eastern Promenade and the fancier Western "Prom," which is lined with stately homes. The Old Port dips to sea level in the middle—and all of it overlooks the islands of Casco Bay.

Originally named Casco when it began life as a fishing and trading village, the name later changed to Falmouth. Falmouth, however, was destroyed in 1676 by the Wampanoags during King Philip's War, destroyed again in 1690, and bombarded by the Royal Navy during the American Revolution.

After this, the "Neck" portion of Falmouth declared itself Portland and the rest is, as they say, history. A checkered history, marked by Nativist movements to oppress Irish immigrants, the genesis and center of Prohibition movement, and a brief fling at being Maine's capital.

The city has been destroyed by fire four times. An Independence Day fire in 1866 wiped out more than 1,800 buildings. The blaze, probably started by a firecracker or cigar ash, was the greatest fire in a US city at that time—five years before the Great Chicago Fire. After

Mistake Island: The Maine coast abounds with places whose names serve as a warning to boaters. This is one of them. Mist enshrouds this island off the coast of Jonesport some 20 percent of the year, making it the foggiest place on the east coast of the United States. President John Quincy Adams authorized the construction of the 57-foot Moose Peak Lighthouse on the island in 1825 to cut down on mistakes of the fatal sort.

Monhegan Island: A Mi'kmaq or Maliseet term meaning "out-to-sea island." Another island with a tiny year-round population dependent on lobstering, and a major tourist attraction in the summer. Reachable by ferry, but no cars allowed.

the fire, poet Henry Wadsworth Longfellow compared the destruction of his hometown to the devastation of Pompeii. Two lives were lost, and 10,000 people were left homeless. As a result of the fire, the Old Port is dominated by low-rise, mostly brick buildings.

About 64,000 residents live inside the city with 230,000 in the greater metropolitan area. Portland is the second largest fishing port and largest tonnage seaport in New England, and is often ranked as one of the ten safest, most livable cities in America.

A national magazine once accused Portland of having more restaurants per square foot than any place in the US. That claim is likely untrue, but for a city its size, it is blessed with a large number of excellent restaurants offering everything from simple classic Maine fish chowder to far more exotic fare from African to Vietnamese.

Despite its popularity with tourists who come to see the spectacular water views, the iconic lighthouses, and the tidy cityscapes juxtaposed with breathtaking ocean views, Portland is different from some other touristy New England seaside towns. Portland's working harbor and year-round working population save it from resembling a 'quaint' imitation of itself.

Mooselookmeguntic Lake: An Abnaki term meaning "moose feeding place." Another theory says the meaning is "smooth when choppy seas," for an area of the lake by the same name which is smooth during windy conditions. Who cares what it means? It's a great word.

Mount Desert Island: The bald granite slopes of the mountains on Maine's largest island inspired French explorer Samuel de Champlain to name the place Isles des Monts Desert, or "island of barren mountains," when he first sailed past it in 1604. The pronunciation has lost some, but not all, of its French flavor over the years. These days the name often comes out as "Mount Dessert Island," as if the mountains were topped with whipped cream. However the name is pronounced, the island is the state's most popular tourist destination, serving as home to Acadia National Park and the summer haunt of celebrities such as Martha Stewart, David Rockefeller, and Casper Weinberger.

Mount Mica: This mountain in the town of Paris has some of the state's richest deposits of precious and semi-precious stones, including garnet, tourmaline, amethyst, quartz—and the largest beryls ever found.

Muscongus Bay: An Abnaki term meaning "many large rock ledges."

Did you know. . .

. . . that Maine has 67 lakes or ponds named Mud, 31 lakes or ponds named Round and 16 lakes or ponds named Duck?

Did you know. . .

. . . that Fort Kent and Wells both lay claim to the title "The Friendliest Town in Maine"?

Naskeag: An Abnaki term meaning "the end, the extremity." As in Naskeag Point in Brooklin marking the eastern boundary of Penobscot Bay. It's so nice when place names make sense. Of course, only if you speak Abnaki.

Old Maid Rock: A pillar in Oxbow, Aroostook County, with an elevation of 693 feet above sea level. Legend says the spirit of a young woman has been seen there wearing a blood-spattered wedding dress. She appears to be looking for a shoe.

Liberty, Unity, and Freedom

The towns of Liberty, Unity, and Freedom in Waldo County probably earned their names because their incorporation took place after the American Revolution, the last war with the British. Or perhaps the residents were trying to outdo one another.

Freedom was settled by a Revolutionary War veteran, and first named Smithton in his honor, but later changed to Beaver Hill. After the War of 1812, the town was incorporated and the name was changed to Freedom.

Liberty, another former mill town, was first called Davistown Plantation, before becoming part of neighboring Montville for a while, and incorporating as Liberty in 1827. It boasts the only octagonal post office in the US.

Unity was first known as Twenty-Five Mile Pond Plantation when Quakers first settled there. That proved to be too much of a mouthful (even though it was located on a pond 25 miles from Fort Halifax) and the name was changed to Unity in 1804.

When the chicken farming that replaced sawmills began to decline, the townspeople of Unity founded Unity College, now the town's biggest employer. Unity is also now known as the home of the Maine Organic Farmers and Gardeners Association, the oldest such organization in the US, which hosts the all-organic Common Ground Fair there every September.

Old Sow: The biggest whirlpool in the western hemisphere—and the world's second-largest—is formed twice a day when the powerful Downeast tides flood through the Western Passage, along the shores of Passamaquoddy Bay near Eastport. Why the name "Old Sow"? The whirlpool makes unmistakable pig-like noises. Old Sow can become as wide as 250 feet and create six-knot currents in surrounding waters. (The largest whirlpool in the world is Maelstrom Whirlpool in Norway.)

Old Town: Derived from the English nickname for the largest Penobscot Nation settlement, Indian Island, which is still the home of the Penobscot. The Abenaki called it Pannawambskek, or "where the ledges spread out." Best known for the reservation and the Old Town Canoe factory, in business for more than a century. Singer Patti Griffin and author Tabitha King (wife of Stephen) were born there.

Ogunquit: A Mi'kmaq term meaning "lagoons within dunes," Ogunquit is appropriate name for a town with one of Maine's rare sandy beaches, a wonderful cliff walk, and many summer tourist attractions.

Paris

Paris, Maine, is the home of the famous Flexible Flyer sleds, the largest and longest operating sled company in American history. Townspeople chose the name Paris to honor the help France gave the colonists during the American Revolution. Before 1793, the town was called simply No. 4 Township. Paris has a population of about 4,793 today.

For a small town, Paris supplied Maine and the US with several prominent politicians. One of the most famous residents was Hannibal Hamlin, who served as a congressman, senator, governor and vice president. Two others could have been named after the town, except for that extra "r": Albion K. Parris, who was a senator and governor and Virgil D. Parris, a congressman.

They said it

"He was a beloved and highly respected man, said by the Indians to be the son of a French father and a mother half French and half Indian. He was blue-eyed and so light of skin that in his own lifetime he was often thought to have been a captive white boy adopted by the Indians."

– Fannie Hardy Eckstorm, writing about Chief Joseph Orono, who died in 1801. The town of Orono, home of the flagship University of Maine campus, is named for him.

Orono: An Abnaki name purportedly from Chief Joseph Orono. Home of the flagship campus of the University of Maine, which is often referred to simply as "Orono."

Passadumkeag: An Abnaki term meaning "rapids over gravel beds." One that people love to use as an example of funny or interesting Maine place names.

Passamaquoddy Bay: A tribal name meaning "place of abundance of pollack" or "pollack-spearer." Many members of the Passamaquoddy tribe live in a reservation at Pleasant Point in Perry on its shores. They were known for their ability to spear pollack. The bay has many islands, including Campobello.

Pemaquid: A Mi'kmaq term meaning "extended land," (peninsula) "Long Point," or "a point of land running into the sea." This "long point" is made up of large smooth rock formations. It's so easy to walk out on them that people often forget the waves can be dangerous.

Penobscot: An Abnaki tribal name meaning "place of descending rocks/ledges." Originally Penobscot was the name of about ten miles of the Penobscot River between Bangor and Old Town. Penobscot is also the name of a county, a town, and the Penobscot Nation of Native Americans who live on Indian Island in Old Town.

Petit Manan Island: French explorer Samuel De Champlain named this island, along with several other landmarks of the Maine coast. He thought the island looked like a smaller version of Grand Manan Island to the north and simply replaced a petit for a grand. Manan is a word from the Mi'kmaq tribe meaning "island out at sea." Petit Manan is one of only a handful of islands where Atlantic Puffins nest in the United States.

Porcupine Islands: These five islands off the coast of Bar Harbor, all roundish-shaped and topped with tall spruce, bear a resemblance to porcupines. Sheep Porcupine Island, like hundreds of Maine islands, was once cleared and used as pasture for sheep. Burnt Porcupine once endured a fire. Bald Porcupine features an enormous bare cliff facing the open ocean. Bar Porcupine is connected to Bar Harbor by the town's namesake bar at low tide. Long Porcupine is just that—long.

Portage: From the French "carry," usually referring to the carrying of a canoe from one water body to another. The French gave it the name, although the Indians did the original carrying of canoes. Located at the northern end of the Appalachian Mountain range in Aroostook County, the town has fewer than 400 residents. It's a popular place for travelers who like outdoor activities and wildlife.

Quoddy Head: A term meaning "pollack." Quoddy Head State Park is in Lubec on the easternmost point of land in the US. West Quoddy Head Light is the easternmost lighthouse in the US.

Robinhood: A sachem who greeted Europeans and signed many deeds in the Georgetown region. Thus the names for Robinhood Bay and the village of Robinhood in Georgetown.

Rum Key: During the days of prohibition, smugglers often transported alcohol from Canada into the United States via the vast, mostly unpatrolled coastline of Maine. At this small island, according to legend, smugglers would arrive with their cargo—often rum—and wait for a light from atop Cadillac Mountain; the light told them it was safe to enter the port of Bar Harbor.

Saco: An Abnaki term meaning "flowing out" or "outlet," pronounced SOCK-o by Mainers.

Sebago: Sebago Lake is the deepest and second-largest lake in Maine, surrounded by Sebasticook Lake, a Penobscot-Abnaki term meaning "the passage river," "the almost-through river," and "the short route." The name of the tributary of the Kennebec River in Winslow, a heavily-used route from the Penobscot River to Quebec that rises in the Garland / Sangerville / Dexter area and flows southward to Sebasticook Lake in Newport, then to Winslow.

Sededunkehunk: The name means "rapids at the mouth." Incorrectly spelled and pronounced Segeunkedunk. A stream in Brewer.

Smuttynose Island: Although Smuttynose Island lies six miles off the coast of New Hampshire, among the Isles of Shoals, the state of Maine claims it. The island's name derives from the piles of seaweed that accumulate on one end of the island, giving the appearance of a large "smutty" nose when looked at from sea level. Smuttynose Island is best known as the site of the murder of two Norwegian women in 1873. One woman was strangled, the other struck with a hatchet. A third woman—Maren—escaped to a nearby island now called Maren's Rock. Maren identified a German fisherman as the killer; he was eventually hanged for the crimes.

Weskeag: Originally called Wessaweskeag, a term meaning "tidal creek" or "salt creek." It refers to the Weskeag River in South Thomaston, colloquially called "the Keag," pronounced "Gig."

Yankeetuladi Brook, Pond: Blend of English, "Yankee," and Maliseet "tuladi" or "place where they make canoes."

Natural World

Up until 25,000 years ago, Maine was covered by the Laurentide ice sheet. The ice, which sat on Maine for more than 15,000 years, was thick enough to cover the highest mountains, erode previous glacial effects, and wear down the previous sediment cover.

When the ice finally receded, the ice carried its sediment south, releasing pulverized rock debris, which either formed a stony deposit called 'till' or washed out in meltwater streams. These sediments, deposited mostly in the river valleys, lake basins, and coastal lowlands, formed the sand, gravel, silts, and clay deposits found near the coast. Receding glaciers also scoured the land and dammed the valleys to create more than 2,200 lakes and other waterways.

Tucked up in the northeast corner of the United States and bordering Canada, Maine has the longest coastline in the contiguous 48 states (if stretched into a straight line, it would reach beyond Florida).

Ninety percent of Maine is covered by trees, making it the most heavily forested state in the country. The land is fed by an intricate network of lakes, rivers, and streams. The nearshore coastal waters are dotted by thousands of islands, small and large, several with year-round communities.

Maine's mountain chain is known locally as Longfellow, but they are an extension of New Hampshire's White Mountains, and all of them form part of the Appalachian range that runs from Georgia to Newfoundland.

MAINE'S CAPITAL CITY IS . . .

- 4,724 miles from Anchorage, AK
- 3,148 miles from Los Angeles, CA
- 3,252 miles from Portland, OR
- 1,143 miles from Chicago, IL
- 534 miles to Halifax, Nova Scotia
- 375 miles to New York City, NY
- 212 miles from Providence, RI
- 170 miles to Boston, MA
- 57 miles from Portland, ME

WHERE IT'S AT

Longitude: 66°57'W to 71°7'W
Latitude: 43°4'N to 47°28'N

The geographic center of Maine is located in Piscataquis County, at Brownville Junction, 18 miles north of Dover-Foxcroft at longitude 69° 14.0'W and latitude 45° 15.2'N.

The capital, Augusta, is at latitude 44°34'N and longitude 69°76'W, the same latitude as Waterbury, Vermont and Nemilsko Brdo in the Federation of Bosnia and Herzegovina.

UP, DOWN, AND ALL AROUND

- Highest Point: Mount Katahdin, at 5,276 feet above sea level
- Lowest Point: Sea level, at the Atlantic Ocean
- Greatest East-West Distance: 202 miles
- Greatest North-South Distance: 311 miles
- Mean Elevation: 600 feet above sea level
- Land Area: 30,865 square miles
- Inland Water Area: 2,264 square miles
- Coastal Water Area: 613 square miles
- Number of Islands: 4,613
- Largest Island: Mount Desert Island

TAKE5 MAINE'S FIVE
LONGEST RIVERS

1. **St. John**, 331 miles with southwest branch and 325 with southeast branch
2. **Penobscot**, 240 miles with west and north branches
3. **Androscoggin**, 174 miles
4. **Kennebec**, 170 miles with West Outlet
5. **Saco**, 121 miles

Source: Length and Breadth of Maine, by S.B. Attwood, 1977, University of Orono Press, Orono, Maine.

STATE SYMBOLS

- State Flower: White pine cone and tassel
- State Tree: White pine
- State Bird: Black-capped chickadee
- State Cat: Maine coon
- State Dessert: Blueberry Pie
- State Fish: Landlocked salmon
- State Insect: Honeybee
- State Herb: Wintergreen
- State Animal: Moose
- State Fossil: Pertica quadrifaria
- State Berry: The wild blueberry
- State Gemstone: Tourmaline
- State Soil: Chesuncook Soil Series
- State Treat: Whoopie Pie

They said it

"*All I could see from where I stood / was three long mountains and a wood / I turned and looked the other way / and saw three islands in a bay*"
– Poet Edna St. Vincent Millay describing Maine's visual contrast of forested slopes sweeping down to the sea in "Renascence"

TAKE 5 MAINE'S LARGEST LAKES

1. **Moosehead Lake** (74,890 acres)
2. **Sebago Lake** (28,771 acres)
3. **Chesuncook Lake** (23,070 acres)
4. **Flagstaff Lake** (20,300 acres)
5. **The Pemadumcook chain of lakes** (18,300 acres)
(For purists who won't consider a chain as a lake, the next largest is . . .)
6. **Spednick Lake** (17,219 acres)

Source: Maine Lake Charts, Inc.

DIVIDED BY THREE

- The Coastal Lowlands, which begin at the Atlantic and extend 10 to 40 miles inland, is characterized by flat, sandy beaches in the south and small, rockier beaches between high cliffs in the north.

- The Eastern New England Uplands stretch 20 to 50 miles wide, from Canada south to Connecticut. This area rises from sea level to nearly 2,000 feet in the west, with the Longfellow Mountains in the center. The Aroostook Plateau, with its deep fertile soil, forms the northern part of the Coastal Lowlands, where Maine's primary farmland is found, and is the home of the Maine potato.

- The White Mountains Region extends through northwestern Maine, spreading from five miles wide in the north to 30 miles wide in the south. Maine's highest peak, Mt. Katahdin, is found here, along with nine other mountains more than 4,000 feet high and 97 being higher than 3,000 feet.

Did you know. . .

. . . that the Maine Guide service was established March 19, 1897, and within one year, 1,316 guides were registered?

Moose

Maine's moose population is estimated at 29,000, more than any state other than Alaska. The majestic Maine moose can stand 7 feet at the shoulder and weigh up to 1,600 pounds. Antlers on the adult male can weight more than 70 pounds and measure 5 feet across.

Moose can carry 100 pounds of food in its stomach and can easily swim 10 miles. They run at speeds up to 35 mph, and their hooves work as little snowshoes to help them move easily through deep snow. Unlike deer, moose thrive in deep snow.

As the largest land animal in Maine, the moose has taken on celebrity status. Maine's tourism industry has seen an increasing number of tour guides and companies setting up shops handling more and more people curious to see the mighty moose.

For many hunters, the magnificent moose is one of the most sought after species on the continent. And it is not only because of their size and the thrill of the hunt, but also because of the succulence of the meat and the yield. The moose hunt in Maine is run by lottery and in 2008 hunters killed 2,202 out of 2,880 permits issued. Although they're fairly non-aggressive and they won't eat you (they're herbivores preferring high grasses and shrubs, sometimes feeding underwater on slimy pond weeds), they can and will kill people – by colliding with cars. Moose are difficult to see on the road at night. Their dark fur absorbs light and they stand so tall motorists usually don't see light reflected by their eyes. When they hit a car, their legs are usually broken by the impact and their huge bodies fall onto the windshield. Since 1995, 33 people have been killed in Maine by moose-car accidents. Annually, such collisions average 700. Peak time of year for moose-car collisions is spring, from dusk to dawn, when they're craving salt found on the roadside. Sometimes they dash from the woods to escape the heat and black flies. Peak accident locations are up north, where there are more of them, but such crashes can happen anywhere in the state.

TAKE5 CAPTAIN JIM SHARP'S FIVE
SIGNIFICANT THINGS TO DO ON THE COAST

Captain Jim Sharp is author of a recent memoir "With Reckless Abandon: Memoirs of a Boat-Obsessed Life." For decades he owned and operated windjammers out of Camden. He donated the Adventure, one of the only two fabled Gloucester fishing schooners still afloat, to the city of Gloucester, Mass. when he retired. Sharp and his wife, Meg, have founded the Sail, Power and Steam Museum in Rockland on the site of the historic Snow shipyard.

1. **Try a unique sailing adventure.** Here is something indigenous to the mid coast region of Maine that you will not find anywhere else in the world. We have an entire fleet of more than a dozen wonderful, traditional, commercial windjammers that go on 3 or 6 day sailing vacations. The sailing novice or professional can enjoy an experience truly unusual in every respect, helping to set sail, steer these often 100'+ old-time sailing ships, swab the deck or just relax and listen to the music of the sea. Our coast is renowned for an array of magnificent, jewel-like tiny islands, a plethora of narrow waterways with scenery so grand it will take your breath. City folk are mesmerized by the wild sea life, the bird life, the moon reflected on the water, a gentle cheek-caressing so'wester, a grand and glorious sea-goin' dinner, or — the red, morning sunrise-- freshly brewed coffee—quiet contemplation of an empty deck. Only in Maine & truly unique!

2. **Kayaking the Deer Island Thoroughfare.** Paddle in the clear, calm, iridescent tide pools between the tiny islands of the pointed firs. Pristine pastures mowed recently by wild sheep roll between the knotted nest of a soft wood grove, their knurled roots clinging with desperation to the lichen covered rocks lapped and polished by the salt wavelets. Alone in your frail craft you can treasure our coast only inches from the sea and stop at personal whim to lunch on a deserted beach or hike to the top of a hill where the vista will astound. Now you know you're in Maine—a kayaker's paradise---'till the old mud fog rolls in.

3. **Pick your own critter.** They say the first man to eat a Maine Lobster musta been some terrible hungry. A lobster may not be the most sightly of sea creatures but they are a way of life for Down East fishermen. If you are lucky enough, roll out of your bunk at 0300, haul on your long johns, sea boots 'n so'wester and take a hauling trip with a true, scaley, crusty old Maine lobsterman. The science of lobstering is worth the getting' up early for and the memory of a early dawn, a great rolling green wave and the seals watching from a foamy breaking ledge, is more savory than perched royally on a $15 platter. Visitors can find, in several ports, lobster boats that take passengers out to get the lobstering experience.

4. **A lighthouse tour can be accomplished by car or by boat.** Portland Head, Pemiquid, Marshall Point, Owls Head, Rockland Breakwater can all be accessed by road and are all worth the effort, but the way to see Maine is by boat. Can't afford your own boat? Leave the four wheels and jump on the first morning Vinal Haven Ferry. When you leave Rockland there will be a lighthouse in sight almost all the way. You will thread your way through a myriad of magnificent tree covered islands, tiny, twisted channels and you'll be awarded a rich taste of our craggy coastal shoreline. Disembark in a small, Maine island fishing village, just as picturesque as a 19th century" hand-me-down." Wander the tiny streets, gaze in awe at the Victorian architecture, the great galamander, lunch at the reversing falls and catch the afternoon return boat home.

5. A piece of history. Maine's coastal waters are steeped in a shroud of sailing history best illustrated in many fascinating local museums. Before the days of trucks, roads and trains, the 1800s ushered in an era of sophisticated schooner cargo carriers that darkened the horizon simply by their numbers. Maine State Museum in Augusta could easily absorb an entire day. Along the mid-coast region, the Lighthouse Museum, Farnsworth, Owls Head Transportation Museum and South Rockland's newest Sail, Power & Steam Museum have more than a week's worth of exciting experiences for the curious mind.

Did you know. . .

MAINE'S LONG, CONVOLUTED COAST

Cartographer and GIS (geographic information services) specialist Richard A. Kelly estimated Maine's total coastline at about 5,300 miles. Indeed Maine's coastline is longer than the length of any other state's coast, except Alaska.

A small part of the Maine coast shares the Bay of Fundy with New Brunswick and Nova Scotia, and therefore the world-record vertical tidal range. Tides in the bay reach 50 feet in some places. In Maine, however, the tides average closer to 26 feet.

Old Sow

Located between Deer Island and Indian Island (and seen from the shores of Eastport), Old Sow is the largest whirlpool in the western hemisphere, and the second largest in the world.

Created by the powerful Fundy tides, it can roil the waters for seven miles around. Most active about three hours before high tide, the current around Old Sow rushes around Indian Island at nearly seven miles an hour and turns right around the southern tip of Deer Island, flooding the Western Passage, forcing the water through the peaks and valleys on the ocean floor.

For two hours, the disorderly water runs from near Clam Cove, Deer Island, to south of the international bridge between Campobello Island, NB, and Lubec creating standing walls of water. Occasionally, especially in spring tides and strong winds, the giant funnel forms up to 250 feet across. Old Sow and her "piglets" can be seen and heard from a few spots on the shore in Eastport. Some believe the name comes from the sucking sounds the whirlpool makes, but more likely it derives from a corruption of the word "sough" which means a sucking noise.

GULF OF MAINE

Scientists once estimated the Gulf of Maine was home to about 2,000 species but the first extensive count by US and Canadian researchers revealed 3,317 species. Called a "Sea within a Sea," the Gulf of Maine is one of North America's most productive marine environments, home to species

Fly Rod Crosby

Cornelia Thurza Crosby was born in 1854, in Phillips, Maine, grew to be six feet tall, became a woman of firsts, and possibly launched the tourism industry in her home state.

Crosby was living the fairly conventional life of a small-town Maine woman when she took the advice of her doctor to spend more time outside. She quit her job in a bank, moved to Rangeley, learned how to hunt and fly cast, developed a lifelong love of fishing, and earned the nickname "Fly Rod." Crosby once said, "I would rather fish any day than go to heaven" and reportedly caught 200 fish in a single day.

Crosby was a contemporary and friend of Annie Oakley, and the first registered Maine Guide. She was also a writer, and Maine's first paid publicity agent (she coined the slogan "the Nation's Playground"). The column she wrote for the *Phillips Phonograph*, "Fly Rod's Notebook," was soon picked up and syndicated in national newspapers, attracting visitors to Maine to hunt and fish.

She attended an 1898 sportsman's show in Madison Square Garden, impressing the crowds with the log cabin she built by hand. She also exhibited stuffed deer, moose, and birds, and a tank full of trout and salmon. She demonstrated her fishing prowess by casting into the tank. "Fly Rod" also scandalized the New Yorkers with her costume, a new lady's hunting outfit with a mid-calf skirt.

Native American and Penobscot ballplayer Louis Sockalexis said of Crosby, "Her face is white, but her heart is the heart of a brave." The High Peaks Alliance in Maine proposes to establish the Fly Rod Crosby Footpath to commemorate her accomplishments. The path would start in Strong, near her burial site, and continue north to her birthplace of Phillips, then to Rangeley and Oquossoc.

such as cod, haddock, herring, scallops, lobster, and flounder.

It is bounded by Cape Cod in the southwest and Cape Sable at the southern tip of Nova Scotia in the northeast. It includes the entire Bay of Fundy and the world's highest tidal variations. The Gulf of Maine and its vast resource of fish was one of the primary reasons for successful European settlement on the east coast of Canada and the US. Indeed many early New Englanders grew rich on the salt fish (cod) trade.

TAKE 5 FIVE MAINE PLACES
JULIAN RUBENSTEIN THINKS EVERYONE SHOULD SEE

Julian Rubenstein, like so many Mainers, has pursued many different interests throughout his working life, usually outdoors. A Maine Guide for many years, he led hunting, fishing, and trapping expeditions throughout Maine and Canada. With a private pilot's license and his own plane, he worked as a spotter for tuna boats. He is also a fine woodworker and a raconteur. His best stories are about his own misadventures, and are reportedly even true.

1. **The Port Clyde General Store:** It's an authentic, old-timey store with the added advantage of a dock on the harbor with picnic tables where people can watch the Monhegan ferry and other boats come and go. The scenery is beautiful, and the occasional celebrity wanders by, for those who care about such things.

2. **Pemaquid Harbor and Point:** This is not the lighthouse park, but another state park where reenactments of historic events take place every weekend in the summer. One involves 17th century European fishermen with the appropriate old tools and apparel. I learned that the captain removed the boat's sails so the crew wouldn't steal the vessel and go home.

Gulf of Maine waters are influenced by the Labrador Current, making gulf waters significantly colder and more nutrient-rich than those found to the south. The Gulf's cold waters encourage the great biodiversity found here. The Gulf is visited by feeding whales in the summer, including the endangered Atlantic Right Whale.

3. **Appleton Ridge:** Drive along the ridge for the view, then have coffee in Searsmont at the Fraternity Village store. The store is named for a book by Ben Ames Williams (a Mississippi writer who summered in Searsmont in which he fictionalized Searsmont as Fraternity). It's a great little country store.

4. **The Airline:** Some of the views along Route 9, a 100-mile road from Brewer to Calais, are spectacular. One is the Whaleback, the prettiest esker I've ever seen. There's a spot on the road to pull off and enjoy it. There are plenty of interesting side trips off the Airline, too. Then before you get to Calais, in Wesley, you'll see the Cloud 9 Diner. Enjoy.

5. If you have a small power boat, you shouldn't miss the area between **Sheepscot and Kennebec Rivers:** Put in upriver from Bath on the Kennebec and head for the Sasanoa River. You can poke up to Hockamock Bay and cross a spot like a fjord with high rock walls, or head down toward Aroowsic under an old iron bridge. You'll think you're in a scene out of *The African Queen*. Goose Rocks Passage across from Robinhood is spectacular. The nicest tombolo (sandbar connecting an island) I've ever seen is in the area. You can walk it, but be sure to get off before the tide comes in.

National Treasure

When the great French explorer and cartographer Samuel Champlain sailed into Frenchman Bay in 1604—sixteen years before the English landed on Plymouth Rock—he can be forgiven for giving Mount Desert Island its rather undeserving name. In one of the most beautifully forested areas of the country, he gave it its Desert moniker because of the bareness of the peaks.

Slowly Mount Desert (the second largest island on the East coast) became a farming and fishing community before being discovered by robber barons, in particular the Rockefellers, Morgans, Astors, Vanderbilts, and Pulitzers, who built what they called their "cottages" (100-plus room mansions that they used for the summer). They in turn brought artists from the city, particularly painters, and particularly the Hudson School, who found in the Maine landscape the same inspiration Turner found in England's.

The rich, of course, have the resources and influence to conserve and protect, and the early days of Acadia National Park in no small measure happened because of their influence. In 1913, President Woodrow Wilson set aside 6,000 acres as Sieur de Monts National Monument. With the acquisition of more land in 1919, President Wilson signed an act establishing it as Lafayette National Park. In 1929 the park's name was changed to Acadia.

When a man of John D. Rockerfeller's means wanted to travel motor free in the heart of Desert Islands, he simply had 45 miles built of some of the finest and most scenic carriage roads ever built in the US. The beneficiaries today of course owe a nod of thank you to Rockefeller for the carriage roads but also for the 11,000 acres he donated to the park.

Today, Acadia National Park contains some 35,000 acres and preserves one of the most beautiful and diverse areas of the country. It includes mountains, an ocean shoreline, woodlands, and lakes. In addition to Mount Desert Island, the park also includes the Isle au Haut, parts of Baker Island, and part of the Schoodic Peninsula on the mainland.

THE ALLAGASH WILDERNESS WATERWAY

The Allagash Wilderness Waterway is a 92-mile-long protected stretch of lake, shore, and river corridor established in 1966 by the Maine State Legislature and managed by the Maine Bureau of Parks and Recreation, Department of Conservation. Set in the middle of a working forest, the Waterway includes a 400- to 800-foot, state-owned, restricted zone within a privately owned forest extending one mile on either side of the watercourse.

TAKE 5 FIVE MAINE BIRDS THAT ARE FUN TO WATCH

1. **The black-capped chickadee** is the official State of Maine bird. Small and very busy, he's easy to recognize because he says his name over and over – chick-a-dee-dee-dee.

2. **The common loon** is a favorite on Maine's many lakes. His haunting calls to his fellow loons can be heard for great distances. At night, many of them will join in a wild and eerie chorus.

3. **Gulls** frequent the seacoast, although more are coming inland as well. These big birds are hungry scavengers and always looking for a free lunch, which they often will snatch out of a beach lover's hand.

4. **The Atlantic puffin** with his triangular multi-colored beak is nick-named the Sea Parrot. Mostly they're found on coastal Maine islands. The puffin's colorful likeness is found on tee shirts, signs, and logos throughout Maine.

5. **The bald eagle** will be taken off the endangered species list after being nearly wiped out in the 1970s from pesticides. Look up and you're apt to see America's symbol making lazy circles in the sky, especially over rivers and waterways, as they look for fish.

TAKE 5 FIVE MAINE
STATE PARKS

More than 30 diverse state parks of various sizes are popular attractions. Many of them include hiking and biking trails, mountains of various sizes for hiking, and are located on fresh water lakes and ponds, and on the shores of the Atlantic Ocean.

1. **Aroostook State Park** is Maine's first state park starting with 100 donated acres in 1938 and now totaling 600 acres through donations and purchases. Its Presque Isle location is a great starting point for discovering the North Maine Woods, the Allagash Wilderness Waterway, and the Canadian provinces of New Brunswick and Quebec. Scenic snowmobile, hiking, and skiing trails.

2. **Cobscook Bay State Park** in Downeast Washington County is surrounded on three sides by the Atlantic Ocean. Cobscook is a Maliseet-Passamaquoddy word for "boiling tides." More than 200 species of birds have been identified in the park and nearby Moosehorn Wildlife Refuge. A total of 888 acres offer hiking and groomed cross country ski trails, boating, campsites, and shelters.

3. **Sebago Lake State Park** opened in 1938 on the shore of Maine's second largest lake, Sebago. Sandy beaches, large woodlands, ponds, and habitat for a variety of plant and animal life make up the park's 1,400 acres. Carved by Ice Age glaciers, Sebago fills a 45-mile square granite basin.

4. **Two Lights State Park in Cape Elizabeth** in southern Maine has 41 acres of rocky headlands providing spectacular views of Casco Bay and the Atlantic Ocean. Twin lighthouses were built there in 1828. One is currently in operation and the other has become private property. Forty acres provide paths along the shore and many individual and group camp sites.

5. **Quoddy Head State Park** is located on the easternmost point of land in the US. Its 532 acres include more than four miles of hiking trails. This is also the location of Quoddy Head Light, a red and white striped lighthouse tower that became the easternmost lighthouse in the US in 1808. The lighthouse is now automated.

TAKE5 MAINE'S FIVE
TALLEST MOUNTAINS

Maine has 711 mountains higher than 1,000 feet above sea level. Many of Maine's mountains are popular year-round recreation sites for climbers, skiers, photographers, artists, and people of all ages.

1. **Mount Katahdin**, Piscataquis County, 5,246 ft.
2. **Sugarloaf Mountain**, Franklin County, 4,237 ft.
3. **Old Speck**, Oxford County, 4,180 ft.
4. **Crocker Mountain**, Franklin County, 4,168 ft.
5. **Bigelow Mountain**, Somerset County, 4,150 ft.

The Allagash Wilderness Waterway was the first state-administered component of the National Wild and Scenic Rivers System. The Allagash runs south-to-north through Maine's North Woods, from Telos Lake to West Twin Brook, at the top of Maine.

Did you know. . .

. . . that Maine's state gem, tourmaline, was the first gemstone mined in the United States? The mining of tourmaline was started at Mount Mica, Maine, in 1822, and with only a few interruptions it has continued producing gem-quality and mineral specimen tourmaline.

Did you know. . .

. . . that Maine's 281-mile segment of the International Appalachian Trail, named for the range that extends from Georgia to Newfoundland, Canada, is considered the most difficult in the US and not to be tackled by beginning hikers?

They said it

LOVE 'EM OR STAY AWAY

Maine's ferocious black flies are immortalized in legend, song, and on tee shirts. The little beasts—females only, of course—have been known to drive huge moose out of the woods at a frenzied gallop to escape their relentless attacks. Maine humorist Tim Sample says the black fly is Maine's unofficial state bird.

A group of wags with the "if-you-can't-lick-'em, join-'em" attitude wear costumes to the annual meetings of their Maine Black Fly Breeders' Association where they tell limericks, jokes, and stories. The group's motto is "May the Swarm Be with You."

The website maineoutdoors.com offers tips on dealing with black flies when visiting Maine, but refuses to take responsibility for the

Did you know. . .

. . . that Maine claims several records for the easternmost points in the US?

- West Quoddy Head (66°57'W): easternmost point on the US mainland
- Lubec: easternmost town in the 50 states
- Eastport: easternmost town of more than 1,000 residents
- Calais: easternmost town of more than 2,500 residents
- Houlton: easternmost town of more than 5,000 residents
- Bangor: easternmost city of more than 20,000 residents
- Portland: easternmost city of more than 50,000 residents

number of bug bites tourists receive. While black flies have no true season, they generally begin biting in May and wrap up by the end of July. Interested parties may record black fly severity at their Maine location on the Maine Nature News site, www.mainenature.org. The scale is: 1) none or few, 2) some, but tolerable, 3) many, a royal pain.

Weblinks

Maine Nature News
www.mainenature.org
A website that invites local clubs and organizations to submit press releases, articles and images related to Maine's natural history; it even has a weekly black fly report.

Maine Department of Agriculture
www.maine.gov/agriculture/index.shtml
Provides information for consumers and farmers on current initiatives, programs, and news updates.

Did you know. . .

. . . that noted American ecologist Rachel Carson did most of research for her book, The Edge of the Sea, at Pemaquid Point? The spot where she conducted observations is now preserved as the Rachel Carson Salt Pond Reserve.

Did you know. . .

. . . that in a favorable year, a Maine sugar maple can give as many as 60 gallons of sap without suffering any effects? Those 60 gallons of sap will boil away to about one and a half gallons of sweet maple syrup.

Weather

The one word that describes Maine's weather is "changeable." Maine's climate is described by weather experts as a humid continental climate; it can be below zero on a Tuesday morning in winter only to be followed by a 58° F Wednesday. Weather and temperatures can vary dramatically from region to region too. It might be snowing in the western part of the state but sunny and mild on the coast.

Perhaps that's why Mainers pay such close attention to weather forecasts and the old time joke is, "If you don't like the weather, just wait a few minutes." Maine experiences a wide variety of weather and some of the widest fluctuations in temperature in New England.

Spring is affectionately known as mud season by Mainers, and with good cause. As soon as winter lets up enough to unfreeze the ground, dirt roads, driveways, and paths become deep with mud. Temperatures range from lows of around 20° F all the way up to the low seventies.

Generally, summers are pleasantly warm, with highs in the upper 70s or low 80s. Expect sweater weather most summer nights along the coast because the sea breezes there can feel quite cool. Usually the daily high for July averages in the mid 70s, but several days are humid and in the 80s. Once in a while, Maine will feel days in the 90s. Variety is the key when it comes to summer weather because there will also be days in the 60s and an occasional day in the 50s.

Fall brings temperatures that cool down considerably. Fall foliage season starts right around the first of October. Frost can hit before the end of the month because temperatures average at least ten degrees colder than July. October nights can be just plain cold. By the end of October, the average temperature low is right around freezing.

Winter varies from year to year but it is sure to be snowy and cold somewhere in Maine during some part of winter. January temperatures range from highs near 32° F on the southern coast to overnight lows below 0° F in the far north.

MONTHLY NORMAL HIGH AND LOW TEMPERATURES FOR PORTLAND (F)

Highs

Jan	Feb	Mar	Apr	May	Jun	Jul	Aug	Sep	Oct	Nov	Dec
24	29	39	51	64	72	77	76	67	56	43	30

Lows

Jan	Feb	Mar	Apr	May	Jun	Jul	Aug	Sep	Oct	Nov	Dec
5	8	19	30	42	52	57	56	47	36	26	12

MONTHLY NORMAL HIGH AND LOW TEMPERATURES FOR CARIBOU (F)

Highs

Jan	Feb	Mar	Apr	May	Jun	Jul	Aug	Sep	Oct	Nov	Dec
19	23	34	47	63	72	76	74	64	51	37	25

Lows

Jan	Feb	Mar	Apr	May	Jun	Jul	Aug	Sep	Oct	Nov	Dec
0	3	15	29	41	50	55	53	44	34	24	8

Source: MELiving.com and absoluteastronomy.com

Did you know. . .

. . . that the difference in the amount of precipitation between the wettest month of the year (November) and the driest month (February) is only slightly over one inch?

They said it

"As boaters, we're lucky to have weather information available in enough formats and media types to suit all preferences. Current weather conditions and forecasts can be found on cable and satellite TV, the Internet, VHF radio, weather radios, and other sources. For the die-hard techie who wants to get weather on their iPhone, there's an app for that!"

– Gail Rice, "Good weather can turn nasty on the water, so be prepared," Portland Press Herald

PORTLAND'S WEATHER WINNERS

- Record high: 102.92°
- Record low: -25.96°
- Record wind speed: 78.06 mph
- Record monthly snowfall: 380.7 inches
- Record one-day snowfall: 21.98 inches
- Record monthly rainfall: 66.31 inches
- Record one-day rainfall: 7.49 inches

YEARLY AVERAGES FOR PORTLAND

- Average morning relative humidity: 79 percent
- Average afternoon relative humidity: 62 percent
- Average precipitation: 43.5 inches
- Average snowfall: 71.0 inches
- Number of precipitation days: 129
- Number of thunder and lightening days: 16
- Number of foggy days: 170
- Number of snow days: 32
- Number of freezing days: 156
- Number of days above 90° F: 5

Source: NOAA

TAKE 5 FIVE MOST IMPORTANT MAINE
WEATHER EVENTS JOE CUPO'S SEEN

Joe Cupo is the chief meteorologist with WCSH-TV, Channel 6, in Portland. He earned a Masters Degree in Atmospheric Science from the University at Albany in 1978 and went to work at WCSH in May 1979. Joe says, "I guess the main reason I've lasted so long is I truly love what I do. Keeping up on our weather is more of a hobby than a job for me."

1. **The April 1982 Blizzard:** On the afternoon of April 6, 1982, the surface weather map showed an area of low pressure off the New Jersey coast. The sky looked threatening but the computer guidance was tracking the storm south and east of northern New England, keeping the snowfall out to sea. Not totally believing the computer models most forecasters did predict some light snowfall but it turned out to be one of the worst forecasts ever made. The storm intensified much more than the models were saying and it tracked right into the Gulf of Maine. The wind-driven snow and bitterly cold temperatures turned April into January and the 15.9 inches that fell stands to this day as the heaviest April snowfall on record for Portland.

2. **The Winter of 1989-90:** The winter of 1989-90 featured one of the most amazing weather reversals of all time. It started in December when an endless series of arctic outbreaks left many of Portland's cold weather records in shambles. The average temperature for the month was 14.1° F which was 11.7° below normal. Not only was this the coldest December on record, it also featured the coldest departure from normal for any month ever. With this shift the arctic air was replaced by much milder air and this new pattern remained in place, making for a very mild January. The average temperature for the month was 30.2° making it the warmest January ever up to that point.

3. **Blizzard of March 1993:** With over 115 inches of snowfall, the winter season of 1992-93 was one of Portland's snowiest. In February, storm after storm came up the east coast. The storm pattern culminated with a terrible blizzard on March 13-14. Called the 'Storm of the Century,'

the snow began in Portland just before noon on the 13th and didn't quit until shortly after noon on the 14th. At the peak of the storm, more than 13 inches of snow came down in just five hours. Total snowfall was 18.6 inches. It was the second biggest March snowstorm in 100 years and helped to make March 1993 the snowiest March ever in Portland with the city receiving a monthly total of 49 inches.

4. **October 1996 Deluge:** On October 20, 1996 a slow-moving area of low pressure was moving up the east coast. As it approached Maine, it managed to tap into tropical moisture from Hurricane Lili hundreds of mile out to sea. This set up the "Atlantic Aqueduct" which led to record-setting rainfall and epic flooding in southwestern Maine. In Portland, the rain began between noon and 1 pm on October 20, and when it ended 48 hours later, a little more than twelve and a half inches had fallen. A total of 11.22 inches fell between 10 pm on the 20th and 10 pm on the 21st, an all-time 24-hour precipitation record. The storm dumped 12 to 19 inches of rain over a 40-mile swath in Cumberland and York Counties. Roads, bridges, and large culverts were washed out in this area along with Portland's main water line from Sebago Lake which left 140,000 customers without water for days. The monthly total of 14.74 inches made October 1996 the wettest October of all time.

5. **The Ice Storm of 1998:** Of all the weather events I've covered since 1979, the ice storm of January 1998 ranks as the most horrific. As warm and humid air tried to push into northern New England, it met with stubborn resistance because this part of the country was under a dome of much colder air. The moisture-laden tropical air couldn't budge the colder and denser air, so it just flowed over the dome resulting in precipitation that started as rain but ended as ice upon reaching the ground. It began on January 6 and continued over four days. The accumulation of ice brought down trees and power lines rendering roads impassable. Half a million Mainers lost power leaving them with no heat, and frozen pipes. Around 2,600 linesmen outside Maine came to help out, but it still took weeks for everyone to get back on line.

WINTER AND SUMMER TEMPERATURES AROUND NEW ENGLAND

Daily average February and August temperatures in degrees Fahrenheit:

Bridgeport, CT	30.4	73.1
Hartford, CT	27.5	71.6
Providence, RI	29.7	71.3
Boston, MA	30.3	71.9
Worcester, MA	24.8	68.0
Concord, NH	21.8	67.3
Burlington, VT	18.2	67.9
Portland, ME	23.3	67.3

Source: Northeast Regional Climate Center

MONTHLY RAINFALL, HOW MAINE COMPARES

Portland beats out Caribou's monthly rainfall record; in August of 1991, Portland had 15.22 inches of rain, while Caribou's record stands at 12.09 in August of 1981. Stampede Pass, WA topped them both with 30.42 in January 1969, and was beaten in turn by Annette, AK with 34.87 inches in November 1958. But Hilo, HI won hands down with 50.82 inches in December 1954.

Maine's driest year (2001, with about 30 inches of rain) in the past 110 years was still wetter than Arizona's wettest year (1905, with about 24 inches of rain).

LET THERE BE LIGHT

- Hours of daylight in Lubec on December 21st: 8:48
- Hours of daylight in Lubec on June 21st: 15:30

Did you know. . .

. . . that the difference between the highest temperature ever recorded in the state (105°F) and the lowest temperature (-50°F) is 155°?

TAKE5 FIVE TOP MAINE
HURRICANES

Maine is a bit far north to get the worst of any hurricane that hits the East Coast, but who needs the worst? Just plain bad is bad enough. Although hurricanes have been noted in diaries since at least the 1600s, detailed records are modern. Wayne Cotterly records all the tropical storms and hurricanes to hit Maine since the days of the colonies on his website and in his 2002 report: Hurricanes and Tropical Storms: Their Impact on Maine and Androscoggin County.

1. **New England Hurricane of 1938:** A Category 5 with winds of 161 mph at its peak, this hurricane hit Maine with winds around 70 mph, causing $135,000 damage (in 1938 dollars), and injuring five people.

2. **Hurricane Carol (1954):** A Category 2 at its peak, its 78 mph winds in Maine caused $10 million, killed three people, and injured seven. One of the worst things about Carol was that she wasn't alone. Ten days later another hurricane hit.

3. **Hurricane Edna (1954):** A Category 3 at its worst, this storm followed on the heels of Carol and caused another $15 million in damages (1954 dollars) with its winds of 74 mph. Eight people were killed in Maine by Edna, and the subsequent floods destroyed many roads and bridges. This hurricane also holds the record of the heaviest rainfall during a hurricane, with 8.05 inches reported in Brunswick.

4. **Hurricane Donna (1960):** A Category 5 hurricane at its peak with winds of 161 mph had downgraded to 77 mph winds when they hit Portland. Rainfall of 3.18 inches fell in the city, with flood surges in southern beach areas. Total damages in Maine costing around $250,000 included dozens of boats and a fire in a Southwest Harbor hotel. The hurricane caused widespread power and telephone outages and destroyed most of an orchard near Lewiston.

5. **Hurricane Gloria (1985):** Gloria was a Category 4 storm at the peak with maximum winds of 125 recorded elsewhere. Maine's 86 mph delivered between 1-2 inches of rain, but caused severe damages. Overall, the storm's total damages were estimated at $1 billion. Fortunately, Gloria caused no fatalities and only three people were injured.

SUNSHINE HOURS

"Sunshine hours" refers to the amount of sunshine there is during the hours of daylight. A higher percentage means there is more sunshine through the day and a lower percentage will indicate that it is likely cloudy.

Portland sees the highest sunshine hours fall between July and August, both at 63 percent. The cloudiest months belong to November at 48 percent, and December at 53 percent.

Portland's annual average of possible sunshine comes in at 57 percent. The nation's least sunniest place is a tie between Mount Washington, NH and Quillayate, WA both at 33 percent, while sunny El Paso, TX leads the pack at 84 percent.

Source: NOAA

IT'S NOT THE HEAT, IT'S THE HUMIDITY

Like much of the northeastern US, Maine can be humid and it can feel pretty darn sticky in the summer. Statistically, however, it's not much more humid in summer than other times of year—it's just that when the mercury hits 90, a high humidity reading is very noticeable. August, September, and October are the most humid months in Maine, and the air is driest in January and February. Like most places, humidity readings are usually higher in the morning than the afternoon.

Did you know. . .

. . . that the 2007/2008 winter was a record breaker? The seasonal snowfall total in Caribou on March 21 reached a new all-time record when the 2007-2008 total of 184.5 inches surpassed the previous record of 181.1 inches set during the 1954-55 snowfall season. By the end of the month, the snowfall total at Caribou was 190.7 inches. (Snowfall records at Caribou began in 1939.)

TAKE 5 FIVE AVERAGE JULY
TEMPERATURES (F) AT 44° LATITUDE

1. **Augusta, ME:** 70°
2. **Bordeaux, France:** 68°
3. **Bucharest, Romania:** 71°
4. **Halifax, Canada:** 63°
5. **Minneapolis, MN:** 73°

THAR SHE BLOWS

Maine has an average annual wind speed of 10.7 mph in Caribou and 8.7 mph in Portland. Countrywide, it is pretty near the middle of the pack. The place with the highest average annual wind speed is Mount Washington, NH at 35.5 mph, and the least windy place is Oak Ridge, TN with winds averaging at 4.1 mph.

Source: Northeast Regional Climate Center

PASS THE SHOVEL

The record monthly snowfall in Caribou, Maine was 59.9 inches in December 1972. But Portland, much further south, beat that record with 62.4 inches in January 1979. Surprisingly, Milton, MA surpassed them with 65.4 in February 1969. Neighboring Gorham, NH beat all three with 172.8 inches in February 1969. However, Blue Canyon, CA passes that with 176.3 inches in January 1952. All had to bow before Stampede Pass, WA with its 192.9 inches in January 1946. But the US snowfall record for one month was 390 inches (32.5 feet) in Tamarack, CA in January 1911.

Did you know. . .

. . . that Maine has the fewest thunderstorm days of any state east of the Rockies?

A 100-Year Event in Fort Kent

The raging St. John River forced the evacuation of more than 600 people when water spilled into downtown Fort Kent in May 2008, leading scientists to call the flood "greater than a 100-year event."

Spokesmen for the Maine Emergency Management Agency said flooding of the town of 4,200 residents was caused when at least 3 inches of rain combined with melting snow to raise the river level to 30 feet, about 5 feet above flood stage, sending the water down Main Street.

On the other side of the river, warnings were issued to residents in all low-lying areas as far away as Fredericton, New Brunswick, nearly 200 miles from Fort Kent, where up to 1,300 homes were threatened by rising water. In Fort Kent, more than 100 homes and businesses were emptied.

The International Bridge over the St. John between Fort Kent and Clair, New Brunswick, was closed for fear the raging waters would drag it down. Witnesses said a local church was flooded and cars floated around in the parking lot.

The previous St. John River record crest of 27.3 feet was set in 1979. The longest free-flowing river east of the Mississippi, the St. John is about 410 miles long, with 210 of the miles in Maine, where it starts. It forms the border with Canada at one section and continues on through New Brunswick to the ocean.

Evacuations took place along the river in Van Buren, downstream from Fort Kent, and in Mattawamkeag, where the Mattawamkeag and Penobscot Rivers both spilled over their banks, according to the National Weather Service.

Weather officials said melt from the six inches of snow still on the ground following a winter in which 200 inches of snow fell joined with the 3 inches of rainfall to exacerbate the situation.

BRR . . .

Caribou is rated as the third coldest city in the US with an average annual temperature of 38.9° F, however, the lowest recorded temperature in Maine was -48° F, recorded on January 19, 1925 in Van Buren at elevation 510 feet, until the record was broken January 16, 2009 in Big Black River, near Caribou. This is tied with the coldest day in New England history with a 1933 temperature recorded in Bloomfield, Vermont. However, the single coldest recorded temperature in the US was in Prospect Creek, Alaska at -80° F.

DREAMING OF A WHITE CHRISTMAS

A white Christmas is defined as having at least one inch of snow on the ground on December 25. If you're in Caribou, you have a pretty good chance at 97 percent, and an 83 percent chance in Portland. If you're hoping for ten inches of snow or more for Christmas, in Caribou you have a 57 percent chance, and in Portland, just a 13 percent chance.

Source: About.com: Weather

They said it

"On the coast of Maine, where many green islands and salt inlets fringe the deep-cut shoreline stood a small house facing the morning light. All the weather-beaten houses of that region face the sea apprehensively, like the women who live in them."
    – The Country of the Pointed Firs Sarah Orne Jewett, 1910

EIGHTEEN HUNDRED AND FROZE TO DEATH

1816 was the Year There Was No Summer, also known as the Poverty Year, but usually referred to as Eighteen Hundred and Froze To Death. Winter was fairly dry for Maine that year, spring was late and dry, but the growing season from late spring to early fall saw a series of cold waves that destroyed crops and reduced the food supply. Snow fell in June, frost hit in July and again in August. Some reports say hail or snow fell every month that year in Maine. The entire Northeast was affected, from New England through Canada; the reason for those drastic conditions was likely the 1815 eruption of a volcano in Indonesia.

TORNADOES, WATERSPOUTS, WHATEVER...

Maine's modern tornadoes, one to two a year, have been generated by severe summer storms, most often in the southwestern and central sections of the state. Due to Maine's rural nature, property damage and personal injuries have been slight since tornadoes usually have touched down in heavily wooded areas.

Maine ranks number 39 for frequency of tornadoes in the US, 39 for number of deaths, 43 for injuries, and 41 for cost of damages. The total cost of tornadoes between 1950 and 1995 was $7,104,690. The cost per person for tornadoes in Maine is 16 cents per year! This ranks the state number 42 in costs for tornadoes per person.

That said, a tornado hit Phippsburg on Thanksgiving Day 2005, causing damage to trees and coastal homes and camps. And in 2008,

They said it

"September 24: Monday, about 4 o'clock in the afternoon, a fearful storm of wind began to rage, called a hurricane...The greatest mischief it did us, was the wracking of our shallops, and the blowing down of many trees, in some places a mile together."

– From the writings of John Jocelyn on the earliest storm of record in the US in Scarborough, Maine (Massachusetts)

TAKE5 FIVE POPULAR MAINE
WINTER ACTIVITIES

1. **Skiing:** Maine has a selection of ski areas and ski resorts unmatched by many other states. Skiers and snowboarders come from throughout the eastern seaboard, Canada, and across the US to ski some of the most magnificent mountains in the east. In fact, the US Ski Team trains at one of Maine's most popular mountains, Sugarloaf Resort.

2. **Ice Fishing:** Maine offers some great lakes for beginners and casual ice-fishing enthusiasts who want easy access to both the lake and other activities and attractions. Maine also has some incredible lakes for serious, experienced anglers who are willing to snowmobile for miles in order to find the best spot. You may also want to consider the type of fish you want to catch. Salmon, northern pike, brook trout, and lake trout (also called togue) are all plentiful if you know where to look.

3. **Snowmobiling:** Maine has miles of snowmobile trails and the sport is popular throughout the state with many competitive events taking place. A highlight is the International Snowmobilers Festival an annual event held in February in Madawaska and Edmundston, New Brunswick. Snowmobilers drive 400 miles of marked trails on both sides of the border.

4. **Dog Sledding:** Dog sledding is a fun way to enjoy your winter vacation in Maine. Maine dog sled tour operators offer trips ranging from a half-day to several days. They teach you the ropes and allow guests to experience the thrill of driving their own team.

5. **Tobogganing:** The Camden Snowbowl offers visitors an opportunity to race down a mountain on a toboggan, and the US National Toboggan Championships are held there annually each February. More than 400 teams from all over the country compete in 2-, 3-, and 4-man toboggan races.

a tornado struck Gorham during torrential July thunderstorms. In 1855, another Gorham tornado received mention in the *New York Times* when it picked up a house and moved it with the family inside, unhurt. The twister did the owner a favor because he planned to move the house precisely to the location the tornado chose. Mr. Niles wasn't so happy about the barn, however, which was taken apart completely and the pieces deposited hundreds of feet away.

FLASH FLOODING AND VEHICLES, A LITTLE-UNDERSTOOD THREAT

The Maine Emergency Management Agency warns that as little as two feet of water can float most cars and small trucks. If a vehicle begins to float, the driver loses complete control. If stalled in a flooded roadway, the agency recommends abandoning the vehicle immediately to seek higher ground. The water may sweep the vehicle and the occupants away. Nearly half of all flash flood fatalities are vehicle related.

On October 21, 1996, up to 19 inches of rain caused very serious flooding in New Hampshire and western Maine. In Scarborough, ME, one man drowned when he drove his car into a flooded roadway. Unknown to the man, the road had already been washed away.

Did you know. . .

. . . that the largest accurate measurement of an earthquake felt in Maine – 4.8 on the Richter – happened on June 15, 1973 on the Quebec side of the border from northern Oxford County? There has never been an earthquake in Maine's recent history that has caused significant damage.

In 2004 a Gardiner man died when attempting to kayak in a swollen stream. Rushing flood water may look exciting to the amateur canoeist or boater, but it has incredible power and may be carrying hidden debris. In 2007, in Limerick, Maine, a woman and her little granddaughter were swept away when they tried to walk through flood water.

Source: Maine Emergency Management Agency

NOR'EASTERS

Nor'easters typically occur between October and April and bring with them strong winds and sometimes heavy rain or snow. Nor'easters are caused by severe low-pressure systems forming in the Gulf of Mexico or the Atlantic and moving up the east coast into New England. If the storm is to the west of coastal New England, the result is usually heavy rain, but if the storm is wet and cold enough and moving over the Atlantic, major snowfalls can result. The name nor'easter comes from the counterclockwise air movement of the storm, which produces intense northeasterly winds in coastal areas.

SOME NOTORIOUS NOR'EASTERS INCLUDE:

- The Blizzard of '93 in March; there was snow, tornadoes, and flooding from Alabama to Maine with damages in excess of $1 billion
- Halloween 1991; more than 1,000 homes were damaged from the Carolinas to Maine
- Ash Wednesday 1962; northeast coastline was battered for five days straight

GROWING SEASON

Because Maine is such a large, coastal state, it has a varying growing season for its green-thumbed residents. In the north, you can count on approximately 110 days, while the more southerly coastal areas enjoy up to 180 days. The last frost usually occurs in May, and the first frost in late September.

CABIN FEVER

Summer is lovely in Maine, but it's brief and we have little time to celebrate, while those long, cold winters provide time for rumination. Therefore, winter sometimes gets more attention. In February and March, towns get together for "Cabin Fever Relievers" to help winter out the door. Mainers go ice-fishing and hold contests for the biggest fish caught while freezing their butts off (and warming the insides with Allen's, perhaps?). Then, there's ice-out. Contests are regularly held in towns with frozen lakes to predict the day when the ice will depart. In other places, they have football pools, or bet on horses. Mainers bet on ice.

Weblinks

Maine's Internet Magazine

www.MEliving.com

Maine's Internet Magazine tells all you need to know about weather as well as events, lodging, dining, and more.

National Oceanic and Atmospheric Administration

www.weather.gov/view/states

NOAA gives weather reports as well as history and statistics.

New England Sciences and Assessment

http://neisa.unh.edu/Climate

Visit NEISA for details on Maine's climate.

Culture

Despite its isolation and relatively small population, Maine has managed the improbable. And that is that it has created a vibrant and rich cultural life that is markedly different than anywhere else in the country. From Longfellow, Henry David Theroux, and Nathaniel Hawthorne to John Ford, the Wyeths, and Stephen King, Maine has inspired and served as an inspiration for generations of artists.

Today there are some 8,671 arts and cultural establishments in Maine accounting for some 30,000 plus jobs either directly or indirectly. In Maine, the creative economy accounts for more than eight percent of the workforce. Culture as an industry in Maine generates more than $1.5 billion in sales annually. Made in Maine, the online showcase of Maine-made products, for example now receives an average of 50,000 visits per month.

From museums, historical sites, libraries, performance venues, and a number of nationally renowned fine arts, crafts, and performance centers like Skowhegan School of Painting and Sculpture, Kneisel Hall in Blue Hill, or Watershed Center for the Ceramic Arts in Edgecomb, this is a state where the cultural sector is dispersed across a broad spectrum of communities.

Maine's sprawling geography has resulted in isolation between north, south, and central, and between inland and coastal areas, which in many instances has served to preserve local cultures that have disappeared elsewhere. So-called backwoods Maine has for generations been a hotbed for emerging artists.

In northern Maine and the industrial cities, French Canadian culture remains strong, with French still spoken and sung in many homes. There is also a strong Celtic musical tradition in the state, and the nineteenth century brought influxes of not just French Canadians, but also Irish, as well as Germans and Finns. More recently, immigrants from Africa and Asia have given Maine a new look, particularly in Portland, where one high school now claims students from over 30 countries.

MAINE'S CREATIVE COMMUNITY

A 2008 Maine Arts Commission survey of Maine's artists shows the breakdown of creative discipline of those who participated in the questionnaire.

- Visual arts: 39.5 percent
- Literature: 16.3 percent
- Crafts: 13.5 percent
- Music: 6.1 percent
- Photography: 5.6 percent
- Film: 4.5 percent
- Theatre: 4.3 percent
- Folk or traditional arts: 2.7 percent
- Dance: 1.6 percent
- Design arts or architecture: 1.1 percent
- Humanities: 0.7 percent

Did you know. . .

. . . that Noel Paul Stookey, the Paul of the '60s hit singing trio, Peter, Paul and Mary, lives in Blue Hill where he has a recording studio in a former chicken coop?

EARNING A LIVING

Maine's participating full-time artists break down into the following income brackets.

No income	4.6 percent
Less than $5K	26.5 percent
$5K-$10K	15.3 percent
$11K-$20K	22.7 percent
$21K-$30K	8.3 percent
$31K-$50K	12.4 percent
$51K-$75K	5.0 percent
$76K-$100K	2.5 percent
More than $100K	2.9 percent

MODES OF REACHING THE MARKETPLACE

Full-time Maine artists are using multiple means of reaching the market-place and audiences.

- Provides or sells art from home: 59.6 percent
- Provides art to a seller or distributor: 50.2 percent
- Provides or sells art on the internet: 32.5 percent
- Provides art education: 36.5 percent
- Performs art to public places: 18.8 percent

Source: Maine Arts Commission

ARTISTS EVERYWHERE!

One wag guesses the number of artists in Maine to be in the millions. With a population of 1.3 million, that estimate might be a tad high, but Maine has an extraordinary array of painters, sculptors, fiber artists, crafters, commercial artists, and graphic and web designers.

The city of Portland boasts hundreds of galleries, while tiny Rockland—halfway up the coast—has more than a dozen in the downtown area alone, with more in the environs.

The Maine Arts Commission lists nearly 3,000 artists, but this count includes only those who participate in its various programs.

Christina's World

Andrew Wyeth never thought he did justice to Christina Olson. She was so strong and tenacious, intellectually curious, and unjaded, even triumphant in the face of the fact that she was crippled and had been so throughout her life. Here she was, her twisted torso, facing the lonely house on the hill.

Christina Olson was a friend of Wyeth's wife and except for the last two months, she lived her entire life in the house on the hill. As many Americans now know the house is located on a hill at Hathorn Point on the coast of Maine at Cushing and the painting became known as "Christina's World."

When Wyeth finally shipped the painting to a gallery in New York City in 1948, he referred to the painting as flat tire. He couldn't have been more wrong. The Museum of Modern Art (MoMA) purchased it for $1,800 and the buzz surrounding the purchase was such that there were line-ups to see it almost from the start. Today, it is clearly one of the most recognized paintings of the 20th century, and valued in the millions of dollars.

Andrew Wyeth is the second of three generations of Wyeths that are part of Maine's cultural landscape. When N.C. Wyeth found a weather-beaten old Cape in Port Clyde in the 1920s, he felt as if he was home. It was here that Andrew Wyeth would work with his father in the Cape that the family slowly renovated.

When N.C. Wyeth wrote to his friend Sid Chase, he could barely contain his excitement about his house in Maine. "If I could translate into color and design the deep note of mournful joy I experienced from lying on the grassy slope in front of our old house, listening to the soft rush of the water on that stony beach, and feeling the soft, salt-laden air moaning in the hollows of my face, I would feel quite happy," he wrote. When he finally got his first one-man show in New York City in 1939, 11 of 12 paintings were from Maine.

He began a legacy that continues today.

They said it

"Life is enriched by aspiration and effort, rather than by acquisition and accumulation."

– Helen and Scott Nearing, Living the Good Life

A GALLERY OF MAINE ARTISTS

In addition to the Wyeths, many of American's most important artists are either from Maine, or spent a lot of time in the state, particularly on the coast and islands.

Winslow Homer (1836-1910): Homer moved to Prout's Neck in 1883, and often used Maine's coast as a subject for paintings. He was an enormous influence on all of the Wyeths.

Marsden Hartley (1877–1943): Hartley was born in Lewiston (as Edmund Hartley) and left the state in 1892 with his parents. He lived in a number of places before returning to Maine in 1930.

Fairfield Porter (1907-1975): Porter, who was both a renowned painter and a critic, lived and worked on Great Spruce Island.

Rockwell Kent (1882-1971): A painter and left wing activist, Kent lived on Monhegan Island, Maine from 1905 to 1914.

Louise Berliawsky Nevelson (1899-1988): Nevelson, the pioneering grande dame of American sculpture, was born in the Ukraine and

Did you know. . .

. . . that while living at Walden Pond in Concord, MA in 1846, Henry David Thoreau traveled to Maine's Mount Katahdin? He documented his journey in "Ktaadn," one of three essays on the state appearing in his 1864 book *The Maine Woods*. Author Paul Theroux calls *The Maine Woods* "one of the earliest and most detailed accounts of the process of change in the American hinterland. Thoreau showed us how to write about nature; how to know more; how to observe, even how to live."

moved to Rockland with her family as a child. She is best known for her sculptures of found art objects, many of which she painted black, others white or gold and which were arranged in crates or boxes. Nevelson was

TAKE5 DAVE MALLETT'S FIVE MAINE
SHOWBUSINESS MOMENTS TO REMEMBER

Singer-songwriter David Mallett is one of Maine's best-known artists. His career spans five decades, starting when he was 11, and he has more than a dozen albums to his credit. Mallett has stayed close to his Sebec, Maine roots, even as he has toured nationally and seen his songs performed and recorded by countless other singers, including Pete Seeger, John Denver, and Allison Krauss. His "Garden Song" is an American folk classic.

1. **12 years old, 1963, Bangor**. My brother Neil and I, with Hal Lone Pine, opening the show for Johnny Cash—holding Johnny Cash's guitar, a beat-up Martin D28, while he did some last minute preparations before running onstage to the intro to "Ring of Fire."

2. **26 years old, 1977, the first Maine Festival at Bowdoin College**. A songwriter workshop with Dick Curless, Jud Strunk, Gordon Bok, and me in a tent under the August day.

3. **29 years old, Lakewood Theater.** The Neworld Review with Noel Stookey and his band, Tim Sample, Eddie Moteau, the Neworld Mimes, and all of us at Lakewood Theater for two nights — the best camaraderie, sort of a culmination of a wonderful idea.

4. **40 years old, Sugarloaf, Maine**. Summer country music festival with Waylon Jennings, Ricky Scaggs, Emmylou Harris, and more. Emmylou says, "You are so lucky to live up here."

5. **57 years old, Prairie Home Companion**, with America's greatest host, Garrison Keillor and his ensemble in Bangor. Slickest production I've ever been in on.

Did you know. . .

. . . that folk singer Don McLean of "American Pie" fame lives in Camden, Maine? Other contemporary musicians who call the state home include ragtime pianist and composer Glenn Jenks, and drummer Jon Fishman of the rock band Phish.

a work of art herself, wearing ten layers of mink eyelashes and wild array of ethnic clothing and heavy jewelry, often topped with a turban-like hat.

Neil Welliver (1929-2005): Welliver is credited with "reinventing American landscape painting." His huge canvases depicted wild woods and barrens in Maine, and he believed his painting was "bridging the gap between realism and abstraction." Born in Pennsylvania, he moved to a farm in Lincolnville, and commuted from there to teach at Philadelphia University for almost 20 years. One museum director called his landscapes "anything but pretty or comfortable."

Robert Indiana (1928-): Born Robert Clark in the state of Indiana in 1928, Indiana was a star of the '60s Pop Art movement. He is most famous for his iconic image of "LOVE" with the LO sitting atop the VE, with the O tilted. First created as a card for the Museum of Modern Art, it was also featured on a US postage stamp, and one of the sculptures of this image can be seen at the Farnsworth Museum in Rockland. For several decades, Indiana has lived and worked in a studio on Vinalhaven Island.

Did you know. . .

. . . that abolitionist and author Harriet Beecher Stowe (1811-1896) wrote *Uncle Tom's Cabin* in 1850-52 while living in Brunswick? Stowe had come to Brunswick with her husband when the latter accepted a teaching job at Bowdoin College. The Harriet Beecher Stowe House, which is not open to the public, is at 63 Federal Street and is owned by Bowdoin College.

Bio Henry Wadsworth Longfellow

With the possible exception of fellow New Englander Walt Whitman, Longfellow was the most famous US poet of the nineteenth century. Longfellow was fabulously popular in his time, and created poetic epics drawn from sources including the Revolutionary War, the fate of the Acadians, and Native American myth.

Longfellow was born in Portland in 1807, the second of eight children. At age 13, he published his first poem in the *Portland Gazette*, and the following year entered Bowdoin College in Brunswick. He graduated in 1825, a member of the same class as the writer Nathaniel Hawthorne (who would become a close friend). Longfellow then spent three years in Europe, but returned to Portland in 1829, married, and took a teaching job at his alma mater.

Although Longfellow would travel the world and eventually take a position at Harvard, he returned to Portland often. His family remained here, and Longfellow came back often for family events and even to write. When Portland burned to the ground 1866 in the country's worst fire to date, Longfellow described the carnage this way: "Desolation! Desolation! Desolation! It reminds me of Pompeii, the 'sepult city'."

It was in the 1850s that Longfellow achieved his greatest fame. In 1861, his second wife, Fanny, burned to death, and Longfellow was himself burned while trying to extinguish the flames. To camouflage the facial scars, Longfellow grew a beard, for which he became well known.

Throughout the 1860s and 1870s, Longfellow, whose poetic output had slowed, continued to be showered with honors, both in the US and abroad, where he was often received by heads of state, including Queen Victoria. Longfellow had an enormous influence on the popular culture of his day. A number of common phrases, including "ships that pass in the night," and "footprints on the sands of time," are credited to him.

LITERATURE

Maine lays claim to many successful writers. Stephen King, who lives in Bangor, is the best known, but the seaside town of Camden is home to two authors with impressive track records as well.

Richard Russo won the 2002 Pulitzer Prize in fiction for his novel *Empire Falls*. Russo's saga of a dying Maine mill town was made into a 2005 HBO movie starring Paul Newman, Philip Seymour Hoffman, Joanne Woodward, and Ed Harris. Newman also starred in the film adaptation of Russo's 1993 novel *Nobody's Fool*.

Russo was born in 1949 and grew up in upstate New York; he typically sets his fiction in gritty, declining blue-collar towns similar to where he was raised. A former professor at Colby College in Waterville, Russo is married and has two daughters. His most recent novel is *Bridge of Sighs* (2007).

Another Camden scribe is Tess Gerritsen, M.D., who first started writing while on maternity leave. She ultimately gave up medicine to write full-time and raise her children. Gerritsen published her first novel, a romantic thriller, in 1987 and followed it up with eight more such efforts.

She then turned to medical thrillers, and her 1996 book *Harvest* hit the *New York Times'* bestseller list. Since then, Gerritsen has written a number of other bestsellers, and her books have sold more than 20 million copies. Gerritsen's work has also been translated into 33 languages, and *Publisher's Weekly* has called her the "medical suspense queen."

Did you know. . .

. . . that the villainous Marvel Comics character, MODOK, was created from the benign lab technician George Tarleton, a native of Bangor? The GI Joe character Sneak Peak is also from Bangor, along with Crystal Ball's mother. The location of DC Comics second "Dial H for Hero" series is a suburb of Bangor.

MUSIC, DANCE & MORE

Maine enjoys a rich, varied music scene featuring everything from symphony orchestras, to the down-home fiddle traditions of the Celtic and Franco-American communities. Country music is popular, and country music stations dominate the radio airwaves. Despite the lack of musical

King of Maine

The word "bestseller" is tossed around rather casually in the publishing business, but it certainly is apt in Stephen King's case. The horror master has sold between 300 million and 350 million books to date. King was born in Portland in 1947, and now lives in Bangor, where his Victorian home is surrounded by a custom-built wrought iron fence topped with bats.

Well known as a horror writer, the prolific King (who also has published under the name Richard Bachman) also writes in the fantasy, science fiction, and western genres. In addition to penning novels, King has authored short stories, screenplays, essays, columns, and non-fiction books, including his 2000 autobiographical effort *On Writing: A Memoir of the Craft*.

Many of King's books and short stories have been made into movies – most notably *Carrie*, *The Shining*, *Misery*, and *Pet Sematary*. His short story, "The Body," was the basis for the hit movie, *Stand By Me*. King has also dabbled in acting, making cameo appearances in some of the film and television adaptations of his work, as well as guest starring on *The Simpsons*.

In 1999, King was struck by a car as he walked along the side of Route 5 near Center Lovell, Maine. King was flung 15 feet and suffered, among other serious injuries, a broken hip and a collapsed lung. King had a lengthy period of rehabilitation, and has written about the accident in both his fiction and non-fiction. At one point, citing creative burnout

Did you know. . .

. . . that Marshall Point, Port Clyde, is the site of the lighthouse Forrest Gump runs to In the movie of the same name?

VISUAL MEDIA INDUSTRY

2008, Maine DECD had a study done on Maine's visual media ustry, based on 2005, the most recent year that all needed federal and :e data was available. The study found that this industry alone created 13 full- and part-time jobs directly, and another 2,828 full- and part-ne were created in response to those direct wages.

- **The in-state film & video sector** produced a direct economic impact of almost $24.7 million. That direct spending produced additional revenue for Maine through indirect and induced impacts. Total economic impact of in-state film and video pulled in almost $44.5 million.

TAKE 5 FIVE MAINE
BLUEGRASS MUSIC FESTIVALS

1. **Ossipee Valley Bluegrass Festival** in Hiram, late July. Features the New England Flat Picking and Banjo Championships.

2. **County Bluegrass Festival** in Fort Fairfield, late July. An annual festival in the heart of Aroostook County.

3. **Thomas Point Beach Bluegrass Festival** in Brunswick, late August. This festival has been running more than 25 years.

4. **Countrygrass Music Festival in Jefferson**. It's a three-day family festival that runs on the third weekend every August.

5. **Blistered Fingers Family Bluegrass Festival** in Sidney. Twice a year – in June and late August – 4 days each time. Some "open stage" performances. More than 30 years old.

- **The in-state television, cable, and Internet broadcasting and distribution sector** produced a direct economic impact of almost $326 million. The total economic impact of this sector was $546 million.
- **The in-state commercial photography sector** produced a direct economic impact of almost $13.5 million. The total economic impact of this sector was $22.6 million.

TAKE5 FIVE MAINE
CULTURAL TRAILS

1. **Maine Architecture Trail:** Travelers in Maine pass through many small towns and villages. A brochure has six specific routes, three emphasizing coastal sights, each explaining the connection between the landscape, the people, and the architecture.

2. **Maine Art Museum Trail:** The focus is seven significant art museums containing more than 50,000 works of art.

3. **Maine Garden and Landscape Trail:** A handy map lists and locates more than 50 gardens – a variety from pocket parks to formal gardens.

4. **Maine Maritime Heritage Trail:** The trail focuses on sites that represent coastal Maine's rich history; maritime museums, boatbuilding schools, lighthouses, and sea captains' mansions.

5. **Maine Outdoor Sculpture Guide:** Three long tours of sculptures are highlighted in a 64-page guidebook. The Seacoast Tour features outdoor sculptures from Kittery to Machias. The Sculpture Garden tour goes from Ogunquit to Mount Desert. The Civil War features towns on either end of the coast; York and Calais. Other tours include walking tours of sculptures in Portland and Bangor.

- The out-of-state film, video, and commercial photography sector produced a direct economic impact of $7.2 million. The total economic impact of this sector was $16.4 million.

Source: ECONorthwest

Living the Good Life

Helen and Scott Nearing bought their self-sufficient lifestyle to Maine from Vermont in 1952, providing an example for a generation of young people looking for a simpler life. Their famous book *Living the Good Life* was published in 1954 and became the bible for "return to the earth" movement that would take root in the next two decades. Indeed the influence of the Nearings was significant enough to push Maine population growth in the 1970s into the double digits for the first time since the 1860s.

Scott Nearing was a well-known economist and professor who had lost his job over his anarchist beliefs and pacifist activities during World War I. His wife Helen was a trained musician who grew up a Theosophist (believing in a universal religion which incorporates parts of all religions) and who was with Indian mystic and philosopher Jiddu Krishnamurti during his enlightenment.

The Nearings built their house by hand, using stones they found in their fields and subsisted mostly on what they grew—some of the time. Critics charged that the couple, who wrote many books together and separately, often left Maine during the winter to do book and speaking tours. Scott Nearing chose to die in 1983 at age 100 by refusing first food, then water, until he slipped away. Helen subsequently wrote a book, *Loving and Leaving the Good Life*, about their years together. She died in 1995. Their home in Harborside is now the Good Life Center.

THE CLASSICAL SCENE

Both Bangor and Portland have symphony orchestras. The Portland Symphony Orchestra was founded in 1923, and is the largest performing arts organization in the state. Bangor's orchestra started in 1896, and hasn't missed a season since. Maine is also a spawning ground for young musicians. The New England Music Camp in Sidney was launched in 1937, and has produced many professional classical musicians.

TAKE 5 FAMOUS MOVIE & TV
FOLKS FROM MAINE

1. **Patrick Dempsey (1966-Present):** Born in Lewiston, Dempsey grew up in Buckfield. An actor, he was popular for his role of Dr. Derek Shepherd (aka Dr. Dreamy) in the TV series *Grey's Anatomy*.

2. **Anna Belknap (1972-Present):** Born in Damariscotta, she's an actress who is well-known for her role of Det. Lindsay Monroe in the TV series *CSI: NY*.

3. **Judd Nelson (1959-Present):** An actor born in Portland, he achieved fame in the acclaimed 1985 teen movies *Breakfast Club* and *St. Elmo's Fire*. He went on to act in many other films, make TV appearances, and to write and produce films.

4. **Linda Lavin (1937-Present):** Born in Portland, she's a singer and actress who appeared in the sitcom *Barney Miller* before starring in the title role of the hit TV sitcom *Alice* from 1976 to 1985. She has appeared in movies, on Broadway and made other TV appearances. Her first movie role was in *Muppets Take Manhattan*.

5. **David E. Kelley (1956-Present):** Born in Maine, David is the well known writer and producer for many successful TV shows including *Hill Street Blues*, *L.A. Law*, *Picket Fences*, *The Practice*, and *Ally McBeal*. His most recent project is the hit show *Boston Legal*.

There are professional ballet companies in Portland, Falmouth, and Bangor, all of which offer classes. There's also the Bossov Ballet Theatre in Pittsfield, run by Andre Bossov, a former dancer and choreographer with Russia's famed Kirov ballet.

TAKE5 FIVE MODERN MOVIES
SHOT IN MAINE LOCATIONS

1. **Message In A Bottle**, released in 1999, was filmed in Phippsburg at Popham Beach and in the communities of Bath, New Harbor, and Portland. This big hit starred Kevin Costner, Paul Newman, and Robin Wright Penn.

2. **Cider House Rules**, also a 1999 movie, which won an Oscar for Best Movie, was filmed partly in the town of Bernard, Bass Harbor, and at Sand Beach in Acadia National Park. This hit starred Tobey Maguire, Michael Caine, and Charlize Theron.

3. **In the Bedroom** was a 2001 melodrama with Sissy Spacek and Marisa Tomei and won the Grand Jury Prize at the Sundance Film Festival. A number of Maine locations were used including Rockland, Camden, Rockport, Belfast, Owls Head, Old Orchard Beach, and Wiscasset.

4. *Pet Sematary* by Maine's most famous author, Stephen King, was filmed in Hancock, Bangor, Ellsworth, and Acadia National Park. While more than 50 of his books were made into movies and most of them take place in Maine, only this and *Thinner* were filmed in Maine. The 1989 film starred Fred Gwynne and Dale Midkiff.

5. **The Whales of August** was filmed in 1987, partly in Portland and Cliff Island in Casco Bay. The film starred Bette Davis, 79, and Lillian Gish, 95, as sisters who had been coming to the Maine coast for decades. Knowing they were near the end of their lives, they try to resolve their differences.

Did you know. . .

MUSEUMS

Maine has more than 85 museums and 246 historical societies – it's a state full of surprises and little known facts, and is a museum-lover's paradise. The state is home to more surviving historical forts than any other place in the US, and you can even visit the preserved homes of Lucy Farnsworth and Henry Wadsworth Longfellow.

TAKE 5 MAINE
COUNTRY FAIRS

1. **Bangor State Fair:** Ten days in late July through early August. Traditional country fair and harness racing.

2. **Fryeburg Fair:** Eight days in early October. Bills itself as Maine's largest agricultural fair in prime foliage time. This fair features a favorite; harness racing.

3. **Union Fair:** Eight days in late August. Well known for its annual Blueberry Festival. Harness racing is found here as well.

4. **Common Ground Country Fair:** Three days in late September. A celebration of rural life with emphasis on organic-produced foods, demonstrations, crafts, and livestock exhibits.

5. **Windsor Fair:** Nine days in late August. This fairgrounds has the makings of an early village with its old restored farmhouses, potters shed, barn with antique tools and equipment; blacksmith shop, and even a print shop.

Raye's Mustard Mill Museum in Eastport demonstrates mustard-making in its turn-of-the-century mustard mill. Get your fashion on at Webb Museum of Vintage Fashion in Island Falls, where they showcase a lifetime accumulation of antique clothing and accessories. The Maine State Museum in Augusta is all about Maine's history and people, while the Penobscot Marine Museum and the Maine Maritime Museum are the places to go for the state's nautical heritage.

See rooms full of mounted rare birds, priceless Native artifacts, and even a marlin caught by Ernest Hemingway at the LC Bates Museum in Hinckley. Nylander Museum in Caribou holds the lifetime collection of geologist and world traveler Olof Olssen Nylander. There are 6,000 fossils, 40,000 shells, and collections of butterflies, birds, and geological specimens.

Wilson Museum in Castine contains a collection ranging from prehistoric artifacts to pre-Inca pottery, ship models to cuneiform tablets, and everything in between. Ride a trolley at the Seashore Trolley Museum in Kennebunkport, or watch a bi-plane soar at Owl's Head Transportation Museum. Take your pick – you'll never get bored.

Did you know. . .

. . . that Artemus Ward was the pseudonym of Charles Farrar Browne (1834–1867), an American humorist born in Waterford? As a reporter for the *Cleveland Plain Dealer*, he began a series called "Artemus Ward's Letters" supposedly written by a carnival manager, commenting on current events in a New England dialect. The letters, which were written in bad grammar with misspelled words, made him famous on both sides of the Atlantic. Browne, who died at age 33, was a friend of and influence on Mark Twain, and was a favorite of Abraham Lincoln.

FESTIVALS AND FAIRS

Maine's rural legacy has resulted in a wealth of country fairs and festivals. Traditional festivals celebrate French and Celtic cultures, Maine seafood and berries, and every kind of music, local and imported. Classic country fairs exhibit animals, homemade food products, crafts, and sometimes feature horseracing and tractor pulls. Come summer in Maine, you can celebrate everything from bluegrass music to eggs, clams, antiques, and Native American traditions. Just bring insect repellent and sunscreen.

Did you know. . .

. . . that John Ford, considered one of film's greatest directors, was born in Cape Elizabeth in 1894 to Irish immigrant parents? Ford, who directed dozens of movies including *Stage Coach*, *The Grapes of Wrath*, *How Green Was My Valley*, and *The Searchers*, attended high school in Portland and moved to Hollywood as a young man. He was a recipient of a Presidential Award of Freedom, and died in 1973.

Weblinks

Maine Arts Commission

www.mainearts.maine.gov

The Maine Arts Commission encourages and stimulates public interest and participation in the cultural heritage and cultural programs of Maine.

Maine Writers & Publishers Alliance

www.mainewriters.org

Maine Writers and Publishers Alliance is a nonprofit arts organization that supports writers and publishers in the state of Maine.

Maine Film Office

www.filminmaine.com

An online resource for companies interested in film production in the state. Here, you can find credits, works in progress, and benefits of considering making a film in Maine.

Food

Maine is famous for food, and food production. Visitors are drawn to the state's iconic lobster fishing communities, but agriculture is big too, notably the extensive blueberry barrens and Aroostook County's blooming potato fields.

The enjoyment of local products in their home setting is a paramount Maine experience. Boil a lobster, mash a few potatoes, and top it off with a blueberry pie or blueberry melt-in-your-mouth, and you're in heaven. Maine also grows plenty of corn too, so the ingredients for a shoreside clambake are close by: clams, lobster, mussels, potatoes, and corn. All can be buried in a pit on a layer of glowing coals and topped by seaweed. Heaven squared.

MAINE FOOD GLOSSARY

Bakewell Cream: A powered leavening agent used in place of baking powder or cream of tartar that originated in Maine more than 60 years ago. It is still made in Hampden and sold throughout New England. The yellow and blue canisters sport the original "no fail" biscuit recipe. Like Lake Woebegone's Powdermilk Biscuits, only real.

Bean Hole Beans: Native Americans, probably Penosbcots, taught early settlers to cook beans in a pot over coals in a hole in the ground. They were a regular feature in early logging camp fare. Many small-town celebrations in Maine still feature Bean Hole Beans. Bean varieties usually used are Yellow Eye, Soldier Beans or Jacob's Cattle. Beans are soaked overnight first, put in an iron, lidded pot that's placed in a hole filled with hot coals about three inches deep. Another batch of hot coals is put atop the lid and the whole thing is covered with dirt and left for eight hours or overnight.

Bean Supper: Public suppers usually held at a Grange, VFW, American Legion, or church hall. The bean suppers obviously feature beans, while others - public suppers, church suppers – feature clam chowder, fish chowder, spaghetti, or a variety of pot luck dishes. All offer other side dishes and desserts, usually pies. All food is prepared and donated by local folks. Usually the supper is a fundraiser for a cause, sometimes for a local person or family who has suffered an injury or a loss of property such as a house to fire, or a boat to sinking, or some other disaster. One of Maine's best bargains in eating out as well as a great social event.

Blueberry Melt-in-Your-Mouth: A popular cake made at home with fresh blueberries, usually baked in an 8" square pan, unfrosted and sprinkled with sugar before baking.

Chowder: Maine, like most of New England, only considers chowder to be milk-based. No others need apply because they'll be laughed out of the public supper. Clam, fish, or corn are the traditional chowders although restaurants increasingly offer seafood chowders that vary in their ingredients. Some of these are thick and creamy, but the traditional Maine fish chowder is made with milk and just a few other ingredients besides the fish, such as onions, butter, and salt pork.

Whoopie Pies

The whoopie pie is enjoying a full-fledged renaissance and can now be found at nearly every convenience and grocery store in the state. And when berries, shrimp, Christmas wreaths, and sea lavender are out of season, whoopie pies are sometimes sold from pick-up trucks by the side of the road. An organic version shows up at farmers' markets around the state, and whoopie pies, which used to be unique to Maine and Pennsylvania's Amish country, have become trendy among foodies in many parts of the US and around the world. Upscale bakeries have often offer the characteristic Maine cake, which was officially designated the Maine State Treat in 2011.

Whoopie flavors have expanded wildly. For years, there was only one whoopie pie; a chocolate cake upper and lower outside, with a filling made with vegetable shortening and lots of sugar. This classic was about three inches across and nearly two inches high (LOTS of calories). New varieties include pumpkin spice, strawberry, chocolate chip, mocha, gingerbread, maple, peanut butter, banana cream, mint, red velvet, oatmeal, and more.

The local whoopie queen is Amy Bouchard, who started baking the confections in her kitchen in Gardiner in the mid 90s as a way to supplement the family income. From a dozen or so hand-made whoopies per day, the business has grown to include a new factory and bake shops in Gardiner, Farmingdale, and Freeport. Bouchard has sold millions of her whoopies so far, and besides a large wholesale business, sells them via mail-order on her company's website.

Bouchard calls the bakery Isamax Snacks, and it is named for her two children, Isabella and Maxx. The trademark confections are known as "Wicked Whoopies" because her friends always said her pies were "wicked." As she points out, "In Maine, when something's good, we call it 'good.' When something's great, we call it 'wicked.'" Legend has it that when the whoopie pie was invented back in the mists of time, it was so named because anyone who took a bite yelled, "Whoopie!"

Clambake: Term for a dinner including far more than clams that is cooked underground at the seashore. Usually involves lobster, clams, ears of corn, and potatoes, and perhaps onions, codfish or mussels – but these are optional. The cooking method involves a hole deep enough to burn a lot of wood to heat the rocks placed beneath it for two or three hours – maybe a couple of feet deep or so. Coals are removed, seaweed is layered over the hot stones, food is placed on seaweed, more seaweed is layered over food and a big old wet tarp is placed over the hole. Much drinking is required while the food cooks for at least an hour. Have lots of butter available – some melted for the seafood.

Fiddleheads: A Maine spring delicacy, the tightly-furled heads of the wild Ostrich fern. Sold in stores for the brief unpredictable period of availability; people fiercely guard the locations of their favorite fiddlehead-picking spots.

Frappe: Northern New Englanders love frappes and fail to understand why people in other parts of the US call them milk shakes. Milk shakes are exactly that: milk, with flavoring. Frappes are milk whirled with ice cream – thick and delicious.

Did you know. . .

. . . that Captain Hanson Crockett Gregory of Camden, Maine, has been credited with inventing the doughnut hole? In 1916, Gregory told the *Washington Post* that in 1847 as a 16-year-old aboard a lime-trading ship, he tired of the raw centers and heavy greasiness of the ship's doughnuts. His solution? Punch a hole in the center of the dough with the top of a round tin box. He later taught the technique to his mother. Doughnuts with holes are cited in print from at least 1861.

Needhams: Sometimes called Need'ums, because you need 'em. A traditional Maine candy made with potatoes mixed with coconut and confectioner's sugar and encased in dark bittersweet chocolate. Legend has it a fiery Irish evangelist, Rev. George S. Needham, was preaching in Portland in 1872 when a local candy shop whipped up a batch of the

You've got Moxie

Moxie, the word and the soft drink, came from Maine. The name is thought to derive from the Native American term for wintergreen, an ingredient in the drink.

The dark, carbonated beverage was created in 1876 by Dr. Augustin Thompson, formerly of Union, ME, while working for the Ayer Drug Company in Lowell, MA. First marketed as a medicine and taken in concentrated doses, "Moxie Nerve Food" claimed to aid everything from softening of the brain to "loss of manhood." Ads said it would provide the drinker with "spunk," and the word has passed into the local lexicon as such, hence to say, "You've got Moxie" is a compliment, meaning you've got energy or chutzpah.

One of Moxie's ingredients is gentian root extract, which may be the "root" of its bitter flavor and aftertaste, prized by its fans, but perhaps the reason Moxie is not as popular as sweeter colas like Coke and Pepsi. Moxie was said to be a favorite drink of Red Sox slugger Ted Williams, President Calvin Coolidge, and author E.B. White, who once wrote, "Moxie contains gentian root, which is the path to the good life."

Moxie was adopted as the official Maine state drink in 2005, and is enjoying a resurgence, perhaps in part due to it being served in bars as a mixed drink. Popular choices include the Country Girl (Moxie and bourbon), the Ninja (Moxie with vodka and orange juice), and the Welfare Mom, which combines Maine's favorite elixir with Allen's Coffee Brandy, the state's spirit of choice.

Moxie fans converge every July on Lisbon Falls, site of a yearly Moxie Festival, which has been running for more than 25 years.

treats. The candy maker attended a service and decided to name the candy for the preacher.

Rolls: Maine doesn't have hamburger or hot dog buns, it has rolls. Hence the lobster roll, the shrimp roll and even on occasion, the tuna roll, all served in hot dog rolls. Fried haddock sandwiches are usually served on a hamburger-style roll.

TAKE5 TESS GERRITSEN'S FIVE BEST
MAINE FRENCH FRIES

Tess Gerritsen is a physician as well as an internationally bestselling thriller writer whose books are published in 33 languages. She lives in midcoast Maine. She is the daughter of a professional seafood chef, and grew up eating some pretty amazing meals. Despite those lofty beginnings, she retains an old-fashioned love of the humble French fry. She has eaten fries around the world, and even admits a sheepish love for McDonald's French fries. Her demands are simple: don't over-season. Let the taste of potatoes shine through. And they must be hot, hot, hot! She's always searching for her next favorite French fry establishment. But for now, these are her Maine favorites:

1. **Lily Bistro, Rockland:** The addition of whole garlic cloves makes these particularly scrumptious!

2. **Duck Fat, Portland:** French fries cooked in—you guessed it—duck fat.

3. **Francine, Camden:** Unusual because of the addition of herbs, and the use of olive oil.

4. & 5. **(tie) Atlantica, Camden and Primo, Rockland:** Both crispy, honest, and delicious.

Tonic: In other places, soft drinks are known as soda. Although TV and migration are taking its toll, in Maine, as most of New England, soft drinks are called tonic.

TAKE5 FIVE FOOD FESTIVALS

These are a only sampling – there are several festivals devoted to each of the berries. In fact, the Maine Blueberry Queen is crowned at the Union Fair, listed under country fairs.

1. **Maine Potato Blossom Festival**, Fort Fairfield, is a week-long festival starting in mid-July when the potato plants bloom. It's also a celebration of Aroostook County traditions.

2. **Central Maine Egg Festival**, Pittsfield, happens over five days in late July. The annual festival celebrates the brown egg industry. Activities include the "Egglympics" and the world's largest frying pan!

3. **Farmington Strawberry Festival and Art in the Park** runs for two days in late July. Staples include food, music, crafts, and family activities.

4. **Machias Wild Blueberry Festival** happens over three days in mid-August in the heart of blueberry country in Washington County. This festival is more than 30 years old and features baking and pie eating contests, crafts, a blueberry musical comedy, and lots of music.

5. **Wilton Blueberry Festival**, Wilton, runs for two days, starting the second week in August. More than 80 events include music, crafts, parade, and fireworks.

Maine's Drug of Choice:
Allen's Coffee Brandy

The official state drink is Moxie, the dark, bitter carbonated beverage that originated in Maine. But the unofficial "spirit" of Maine is a 60-proof bittersweet coffee brandy.

Allen's Coffee Brandy has been the best-selling liquor in Maine for more than 20 years, and is so popular a Maine reporter once suggested putting it on the back of the Maine state quarter. One emergency room doctor said it should be on some people's headstones.

In 2008, Mainers bought over one million bottles of Allen's, representing $12.8 million in sales, up 39,000 bottles and $600,000 over 2007. Four sizes of the drink made the state's top 10 list of best-selling alcoholic beverages, coming in first, third, sixth, and seventh. No other brand appears more than once.

Anecdotal evidence suggests that a high percentage of Allen's drinkers are women, and one of the drink's unflattering nicknames is "fat ass in a glass." Also known as a double-wide in reference to "trailer drinks." One woman, new to a neighborhood, told a friend she was impressed by the day-long, relaxed friendliness of a local store owner. The friend replied, "You'd be friendly and relaxed, too, if you were sucking on Allen's all day. What do you think is in that coffee mug?"

Allen's popularity comes from the price, which is low, the sweetness that makes it more palatable than other spirits to some, and the fact that it can be hidden in the morning coffee. Some in law enforcement believe it contributes to crime because of its potency and the caffeine keeps people awake, allowing them to act on their reduced inhibitions. Medical professionals deny this, saying alcohol is the problem, and if coffee brandy wasn't available, its drinkers would simply turn to something else.

They said it

"You smile sardines. The crease these scissors have worn moves into your palm like a lifeline. And more, your apron full of the stench of fish, the torsos packed into oil and canned, bears your body home, smothered in scales of pearls."

– Kathleen Lignell Ellis in an excerpt from "In the Sardine Factory," from *Maine Speaks: An Anthology of Maine Literature*

MOMMA BALDACCI'S: FOOD PLUS

How many governors can say they practically grew up in a restaurant? Maine's governor, John Baldacci, can and does. His father and mother, Robert and Rosemary, when they opened Momma Baldacci's in Bangor in 1974, continued a family tradition that began a generation earlier with a restaurant in Baltimore, Maryland.

Their eight children all worked in the restaurant growing up, bussing tables, preparing the Italian-American food, managing, waiting on tables, and washing dishes. Along with the food and a work ethic, the Baldaccis instilled a sense of public service and civic concern. Their son Paul loved a good political discussion, so when he took over the restaurant, it became a political center. Election nights are crazy there.

When his brother, John, became a politician, it was a logical place to hold fundraisers. The spaghetti dinners achieved fame throughout the state, especially when then-US Congressman, John, took them on the road – a first in the nation. He hosted spaghetti dinners around the state's second district, the largest east of the Mississippi, to listen to constituents' concerns.

Today, the spaghetti dinners at the popular Bangor restaurant, now run by Paul's son, Paul Baldacci Jr., are often held for charity. Volunteers who are sometimes observed serving food at the events include the governor and Maine's most famous resident, Stephen King.

TAKE 5 GRIFFIN MEARA'S FIVE FAVORITE
PLACES TO GO OUT WITH FRIENDS
IN PORTLAND

Griffin Meara was born in Boston, moved to Maine at age 2, grew up in Camden, moved to Portland 22 years ago, and has worked in the food industry ever since. She worked for 12 years at the recently-closed Big Mama's and a variety of other places as a cook, waitress and bartender, including Jones Landing on Peaks Island and Bintliff's American Cafe. She's currently working at Shay's Grill Pub.

1. **Ruski's** serves breakfast, lunch and dinner until almost closing time, and though it's small, they occasionally have great live music. A comfortable neighborhood pub.

2. **Local 188** has a huge tapas menu and wine list along with salads and entrees, and the food is consistently great. The tapas make it an awesome place to go in a group so everyone can share.

3. Along the same lines for groups, but far more affordable, is **Tu Casa**, a tiny family-run Salvadoran restaurant on Washington Avenue. Portions are huge and cheap, but with such a small staff it usually takes a while, so bring good company.

4. For fresh, local seafood, there is no better place than **Street and Company**. No meat on this menu (except for appetizers), they focus their talents on fish. Their signature dish, Sole Francais, will make your mouth water and maybe even haunt your dreams, it's so good.

5. My other personal favorite is **Ribollita's**. It is a classic Italian restaurant in the East End of Portland with two tiny dark dining rooms that make it perfect for a date or to bring a few close friends. All the pasta is handmade and I have never ever had one complaint about a meal, and I've been going there for years.

TAKE**5** FIVE MAINE
COFFEE ROASTERS

1. **Shipwreck Coffee Company**, Veazie
2. **Rock City Coffee Roasters**, Rockland
3. **Carrabassett Coffee Company**, Kingfield
4. **Carpe Diem,** North Berwick
5. **Rooster Brothers**, Ellsworth

PAT'S PIZZA, A MAINE TRADITION

Maine has many independent restaurants, but not many family-owned chains of restaurants. Pat's Pizza is an exception.

Started in Orono as Farnsworth's Cafe by C.D. "Pat" Farnsworth in 1931, selling mostly ice cream and confections, the cafe soon became a full-service restaurant. In 1953, Pat added to the menu a fresh dough pizza topped by a special sauce he and wife Fran developed.

The pizza proved so popular, especially with students at the nearby campus of the University of Maine, that he changed the name to Pat's Pizza. Today, the family-oriented, casual dining restaurants are found at 13 locations all over the state and are still popular as ever with UMaine students.

Did you know. . .

. . . that Martha Stewart, inside trader and home decorator extraordinaire, has a home in Seal Harbor? Stewart's three-storey twelve-bedroom pink granite house on Mount Desert Island was built in 1925 and once belonged to the Ford family of automotive fame. The house has been used in many articles in *Martha Stewart Living Magazine*, and also inspired a line of furniture.

IN VINO, VERITAS

Some Maine wineries use the traditional grapes to make their wine, while others make only fruit wines, using blueberries, cranberries, blackberries, strawberries, as well as apples and pears. Others make a combination of grape and other fruit wines. Some use grape juice they bring in, others grow their own grapes, and some do a little of each.

It's a mixed bag, but an interesting array of award-winning products. Add to the eclecticism the fact that at least one winery also has a brewery, while another also makes gin and rum! Remember, winters are long.

TAKE5 FIVE SCENIC
LOBSTER POUNDS

At these casual, come-as-you-are eateries, lobster comes with a spectacular view (except, of course, when the fog rolls in). Order at the window, grab a picnic table, and prepare for a feast.

1. **Chauncey Creek Lobster Pier**, Kittery Point. This gem is hidden away on a bend in the road, with tables overlooking the saltwater creek and woods.

2. **The Lobster Shack at Two Lights**, Cape Elizabeth. A tradition since the 1920s, it lies in the shadow of Cape Elizabeth Light overlooking Casco Bay.

3. **Muscongus Bay Lobster**, Round Pond (Pemaquid Peninsula). It's hard to match this quintessential Maine harbor view.

4. **Miller's Lobster**, Spruce Head (St. George Peninsula). This pound juts into a tiny harbor, surrounded by fishing boats, and features sunsets to die for.

5. **Waterman's Beach Lobster**, South Thomaston. This one's a James Beard Award winner situated on a Penobscot Bay cove looking toward the Mussel Ridge Channel. Save room for dessert.

BREWERIES

- Number of breweries in Maine: 52 (20th in U.S.)
- Maine breweries per 100,000 adult state residents: 5.2
- Barrels of craft beer produced 2014: 289,646
- Economic impact: $432 million
- Rose from 34 breweries in 2011

Source: Brewers Association

TAKE5 FIVE FESTIVALS DEVOTED TO
FISHING & SEAFOOD

1. **Maine Lobster Festival**, Rockland, is always held the first weekend in August. This granddaddy of Maine fisheries festivals – more than 60 years old – celebrates the state's primary seafood catch in the place where most Maine lobsters are caught, Knox County. Inexpensive lobster dinners from the world's largest lobster cooker, craft tents, a carnival, all kinds of musical entertainment, crate races for kids, a parade, naval vessels, and the crowning of the Maine Sea Goddess are all found here.

2. **Boothbay Harbor Fishermen's Festival** kicks off the season in late April with the first crate race of the year, a codfish relay race, dory bailing competitions, arts and crafts show, a fish fry, and the Miss Shrimp Princess pageant.

3. **Yarmouth Clam Festival** in mid-July includes a parade, a juried craft show, free music, sports contests, an art show, carnival, sports contests, and clams to eat in every form at the festival's food court.

4. **Fishermen's Day**, Stonington, is a festival held in mid-July on the Stonington Fish Pier and includes a codfish relay race, Coast Guard demonstrations, many family activities, and Wacky Rowboat Races.

5. **Maine Salmon Festival**, Eastport, celebrates the farmed Atlantic salmon industry every September. Music, arts and crafts, chowder, salmon pen tours, and salmon dinners always keep people entertained.

HUNTIN' AND FISHIN'

Residents and tourists like to be active participants in the food chain, and may opt for catching some of their grub by fishing (striped bass, salmon, and trout are biggies) or hunting (moose, deer, wild turkeys,

TAKE5 FIVE PLACES TIM WATTS
LOVES TO HAVE LUNCH

Tim Watts, a native of Tenants Harbor, has owned and operated the East Wind Inn and restaurant on the shore in his hometown since 1975. He bakes many of the desserts for the restaurant, where Jamie Wyeth's artwork lends atmosphere to the harbor view dining room.

1. **Friars' Bakehouse**, Central Street, Bangor, is run by Franciscan monks. Their schedule changes depending on the religious responsibilities of brothers Don and Ken, so it's a great idea to call in advance. Their Whoopie Pies were chosen Best in Maine in a newspaper poll. The tiny restaurant is filled with the aroma of their freshly baked breads, cookies, and muffins. The fresh soups are delicious, as are the hearty sandwiches.

2. **Lobster Pound Take Out**, on Rt. 1 next to the Islesboro Ferry in Lincolnville, is a wonderful place to stop for a restful lunch with fabulous water views. Their seafood is some of the freshest around, prepared in the true Maine tradition. They offer an extensive menu of seafood, and hamburgers for those who may not be in a seafood mood. For me, the choice between a lobster roll and a clam basket is nearly impossible to make.

3. **Morse's Kraut Haus**, North Route 220, Waldoboro. Breakfast and lunch are served daily (except Wednesday) from 9 am until 4 pm. Seating is very limited. Their soups defy description, and I remember

ducks). Whether searching for a meal in the water or on solid ground, the intrepid outdoorsman (or woman) must be licensed and observe the designated seasons.

eating macaroni and cheese, the likes of which I haven't tasted any-where else. Pastries and breads are baked fresh daily. After eating, browse the shop with its extensive selection of German imports, hams, cheese, and sausages, and in season, the sauerkraut made there since 1918. They will pack sauerkraut and their special pickles in the quantity you'd like. It's well worth the drive!

4. **Maelily & Ryleigh's**, 949 Forest Avenue, Portland, is a gem of a small neighborhood eatery with simple but well-prepared offerings. Each day the list of specials—posted on a board as you enter—boasts better-than-home items. Service is usually fast and always friendly. Ice cream is available. Minutes from downtown Portland.

5. **Big Sky Bakery**, 536 Deering Avenue, Portland, serves lunch daily from 11 am – 3:30 pm. This is the place when I feel like indulging in a hearty sandwich on rich fresh bread. Their sandwiches and fresh soups are simple and delicious. They frequently have decadent Whoopie Pies, and a mouth-watering selection of giant cookies. Their homemade granola alone is worth a stop, but do buy more than one bag! Bread Head Club members get cards punched and receive a free loaf of bread after purchasing 12 loaves. I usually stock up when in Portland and find their bread freezes exceptionally well.

TAKE 5 DIANE COWAN'S FIVE
MAINE LOBSTER WEIGHTS AND MEASURES

Diane Cowan of Friendship lives as close to her lobsters as possible without being underwater. Diane has a PhD in biology and has been studying lobsters for 27 years. She founded The Lobster Conservancy and is currently its executive director. For years she wrote a column for a fisheries newspaper called "Ask the Lobster Doc."

1. **45 pounds:** The record size lobster. Lobsters continue to grow throughout life and theoretically, there is no limit to how big a lobster can get. The largest lobster I ever held in my arms weighed 18.5 pounds and was more than three feet long from claws to tail. I can't begin to imagine how one would grip a 45 pound lobster. If I meet one when I'm diving on the bottom, I plan to saddle it up and go for a gallop!

2. **10 years:** The average time it takes for a lobster to reach sexual maturity. Lobsters take a long time to grow up! Lobster mothers brood embryos for 9-13 months, then the little lobsters hatch as larvae that live in the open waters for a few months after which they settle to the bottom where lobsters live and grow for the rest of their lives.

3. **100 years:** The maximum life expectancy for lobsters. When I moved to the Friendship lobster pound in 1999, I tagged some lobsters that I figured were about my age at the time. Now I'm keeping an eye on them to see who outlives whom.

4. **260 years:** Maine's trap fishery for lobsters began around 1850. Before that, lobsters were harvested using gaff hooks and hoop nets set by hand from dories. Things certainly have changed a lot since then!

5. **1.25 – 5 inches:** Maine lobstermen use a "gauge" to measure the length of the lobster from behind the eye to the end of the body shield where it meets the tail. Maine law requires that lobsters weighing less than a pound or more than about four pounds be returned to Maine waters when they come up in traps. It would be difficult to weigh every lobster that came aboard a Maine lobster boat thus the use of the gauge. Size limits help insure that there are plenty of lobsters left in the sea to reproduce.

Did you know. . .

. . . that Maine has the only cannery in the world that packs dandelion greens? Although Mainers can find plenty of the young shoots to pick from their lawns in spring, W.S. Wells & Sons in Wilton can't count on a sufficient wild supply of the weeds, so they have to farm them! Besides dandelions, Wells is the only factory in the US packing fiddleheads and beet greens. Wells has produced its Belle of Maine brand for more than 90 years.

Did you know. . .

. . . that the world's longest lobster roll was unveiled June 7, 2009 at Portland's Old Port Festival? Trying for the Guinness World Records, the roll was cut into 4" segments and sold to support a kids' swimming program. Linda Bean's lobster company supplied the 45 pounds of lobster meat. The roll was contributed by Amato's, a Portland-based Italian bakery and chain of sand-wich/ pizza shops. The lobster roll measured 61 feet, 9.5 inch-es. Observers from Rockland, "Lobster Capital of the World," promised to capture the title from Portland in the future.

Did you know. . .

. . . that two varieties of plum, the McLaughlin and the Penobscot, were first identified in the garden of John McLaughlin of Bangor in 1846? By the 1850s, the McLaughlin had become the most prom-inent American-cultivated plum, renowned for rich and luscious flavor, according to the *Magazine of Horticulture*.

Did you know. . .

. . . that the Burnham & Morrill Company opened a cannery in 1836, canning lobsters for the first time in the state? These days, the company, now known as B&M, is known for its canned baked beans, produced in Portland. And the factory building sports a color-fully lit tree on its roof every Christmas that can be seen for miles.

Economy

The Maine economy today closely resembles that of the nation, with an evolving concentration in the service and technology industries. The resource economy is still vital to the state and as goes the price of those resources so goes the state. Fishing, forestry, paper manufacturing, lumber and wood manufacturing, and boat building still form the backbone of many communities.

Maine's natural resource-based industries have been joined by biotechnology, financial services, high-tech manufacturing, and telecommunications-based businesses. Companies like National Semiconductor, Fairchild Semiconductor, General Dynamics, America, Pratt & Whitney, The Jackson Laboratory, L.L. Bean, and UnumProvident have all taken up residence in the state.

As global competition has erased jobs across New England, other industries like financial services, for example, have grown significantly. Whereas textile manufacturing used to account for almost six percent of the economy 15 years ago, it now accounts for less than one percent. The reverse is the case in the financial services sector. The sector now accounts for $1.4 billion in wages for a total of 5.7 percent of wage and salary employment in the state. Employment in the sector is growing at twice that of other employment.

Maine's unspoiled coast and lifestyle have seen tourism numbers go through the roof and indeed tourism is now Maine's second largest industry behind healthcare. Its share of the state GDP is almost triple that of its sister states in New England.

The Maine lifestyle continues to be a draw for companies and workers locating to the state. The state was rated as the best state to raise a child in a report by the Children's Rights Council, and is a national leader in primary and secondary education. The state has the second-lowest infant mortality rate, the sixth-best prenatal care in the nation, and is ranked 11th in the nation in number of community hospitals per capita.

The Maine workforce has a national reputation for ingenuity and hustle. A University of Southern Maine's Center for Business and Economic Research found that Maine workers are dedicated to improving and expanding training, skills, and education in order to stay on the cutting-edge of today's knowledge-based economy.

GROSS DOMESTIC PRODUCT

Gross Domestic Product (GDP) is the value added in production by labor and property in a state. A fundamental measure of economic health, GDP is the primary indicator of the extent to which an economy is growing or in recession. The sum of value added in all industry sectors equals the GDP.

• Maine GDP: $48 billion

Did you know. . .

. . . that commercial sellers of blueberries must keep records of transactions and pay the state 1.5 cents per pound ($1.50 per 100 pounds) of the fruit sold each season?

You Said How Much?

Median hourly wages for some Maine jobs.

Telecommunications	$24.04
Rail Transportation	$22.43
Investment & Related Activity	$22.00
Utilities	$21.68
Postal Service	$21.46
Funds, Trusts & other Financial Vehicles	$21.29
Internet Publishing and Broadcasting	$21.25
Hospitals	$20.18
Air Transportation	$20.13
Paper Manufacturing	$19.25
Computer and Electronic Product Mfg	$18.29
Truck Transportation	$16.22
Construction of Buildings	$15.77
Machinery Manufacturing	$15.68
Printing and Related Support Activities	$14.32
Forestry and Logging	$14.14
Motor Vehicle and Parts Dealers	$14.10
Apparel Manufacturing	$13.51
Electronics and Appliance Stores	$13.20
Scenic and Sightseeing Transportation	$12.77
Food Manufacturing	$12.14
Sound Recording Industry	$11.76
Furniture and Home Furnishings Stores	$11.65
Personal and Laundry Services	$10.09
General Merchandise Stores	$9.68
Food and Beverage Stores	$9.12
Gasoline Stations	$8.76
Food Services and Drinking Places	$8.61

Source: Maine Department of Labor

TAKE 5 CHARLES COLGAN'S FIVE THINGS
PEOPLE THINK THEY KNOW
ABOUT THE MAINE ECONOMY

Charles Colgan is a Professor of Public Policy and Management in the Muskie School of Public Service at the University of Southern Maine. He has been studying the Maine economy for more than thirty years.

1. **The largest industry is tourism:** Actually, it's health care and social services. In 2007, tourism accounted for about 80,000 jobs, but health care accounted for 100,000 jobs. If you measure the industries by what they contribute to total output in Maine (the Gross Domestic Product), health care is substantially larger than tourism. In 2007, health care contributed $5.8 billion to the state's GDP, while tourism contributed $2.8 billion.

2. **The largest manufacturing industry is paper:** If pulp and paper is combined with wood products as the "forest products" industry, it is still the largest industry in terms of output (2007 total of $1.4 billion) and employment (14,000). But pulp and paper alone is now smaller than ship and boat building. In 2007 ship and boat building accounted for 8,700 employees and $1.1 billion in output, compared with 8,500 in pulp and paper and $0.9 billion in output. The ship and boat building industry is dominated by Bath Iron Works, but a large number of boat yards building very high-end recreational boats make up a good share of this industry as well.

3. **Maine is a "rural state":** Maine sure looks rural. It has by far the lowest population density east of the Mississippi. But economically, Maine is very much an urban state. Two thirds of the state's GDP originates in its three metropolitan areas of Bangor, Lewiston-Auburn, and Portland. Almost half the state's output originates in the

Portland metro area. If the smaller urban areas such as Augusta and Waterville are included, the urban portion of the state's economy is closer to three quarters. The landscape may still look rural, but Maine, like the rest of the US, makes its living in its cities.

4. **Maine is the "oldest state" in the nation:** With a median age in 2007 of 41.1, compared with a US median age of 36.4, Maine is indeed the oldest state in the nation. But the reason is not just because there are more old people in Maine. In 2007, the population over 65 made up 15 percent of the population, compared with 12 percent in the US, but the population under 24 made up only 24 percent of the population in Maine compared with 28 percent in the US. Maine's lack of young people pushes us to the top of the age chart.

5. **Southern Maine is the "Quebec Riviera":** Canadians still flock to Old Orchard Beach and Kennebunk Beach, but Maine's connections to Canada are much deeper than that. Much of Quebec's oil is landed by tanker at Portland and shipped via pipeline to Montreal. As a result, Portland is the second largest oil port on the US east coast. I-95 and the Maine Turnpike provide the major road access between Maritime Canada and the US. And the Auburn truck-rail transfer facility makes Maine a major link in moving goods from Vancouver to the east coast.

TAKE5 FIVE MAINE STATE
EMPLOYEE SALARIES

1. **Attorney General**; $90,438
2. **Chief Justice, State Supreme Court**; $138,294
3. **Governor**; $70,000
4. **Maine State Police Trooper**; $41,000
5. **Secretary of State**; $71,302

Source: Government of Maine

PER CAPITA

- New England GDP per capita in dollars: $44,603
- US GDP per capita in dollars: $38,020
- US GDP growth over 2006: 2.0 percent

Source: US Bureau of Economic Analysis

PERSONAL INCOME TAXES

Maine collects income taxes from its residents utilizing four tax brackets.

- 2 percent on the first $4,850 of taxable income
- 4.5 percent on taxable income between $4,851 and $9,700
- 7 percent on taxable income between $9,701 and $19,450
- 8.5 percent on taxable income of $19,451 and above

TAKE5 TOP FIVE MAINE EMPLOYERS
BY NUMBER OF EMPLOYEES

1. **Hannaford Bros.** (7,501 to 8,000)
2. **WalMart / Sam's Club** (7,001 to 7,500)
3. **Maine Health** (6,501 to 7,000)
4. **Bath Iron Works Corp.** (5,001 to 5,500)
5. **L.L. Bean, Inc.** (4,001 to 4,500)

Source: Maine Department of Labor

L.L. Bean—The Best Known Name in Maine

Before Leon Leonwood Bean opened a store, he had created a waterproof boot for hunters that sported a lightweight leather upper and a rubber bottom. He printed a brochure, obtained a list of nonresident Maine hunting license-holders and started a mail order business. By 1912, he had a four-page catalog selling the "Bean Boot" or, as he called it, the Maine Hunting Shoe, manufactured in his brother's basement in Freeport.

The company's famous money-back guarantee started then, too. Nearly 90 percent of the original batch of boots was returned for a design defect. Bean refunded all the money, corrected the flaw, and continued to sell. Bean's still offers the no-questions-asked, full guarantee of its products.

The boot is still an important part of the company's business and image, and a giant replica of the boot stands outside the Freeport store now. The main building, opened in 1917, once sported simple oiled hardwood floors and counters laden with boots, fishing lures, and racks of rugged outdoor wear. Now there's a decorative fishpond and a coffee bar.

Another thing hasn't changed. The main store has been open seven days a week, 24 hours a day since 1951. The hours were established to accommodate hunters and fishermen from out-of-state who drive through Maine at all hours en route to remote fishing and hunting camps. The store closed only for two Sundays in 1962 when Maine's "blue laws" changed. Townspeople quickly took a vote to reopen the store.

From the one store in Freeport, the company now operates more than three dozen retail and outlet stores, including nine in Japan. Annual sales for L.L. Bean now reach almost $1.5 billion.

CORPORATE INCOME TAX (2008)

- Tax Rates: 3.5 – 8.93 (or the Maine Alternative Minimum Tax)
- Tax Brackets: $25,000 to $250,000

Source: Federation of Tax Administrators

SALES TAX

- Maine's general sales tax rate: 5 percent
- Rate of tax charged on lodging and prepared food: 7 percent
- Rate of tax on short-term auto rentals: 10 percent

The US has no federal sales tax and the state sales taxes vary widely. Neighboring New Hampshire has no sales tax, so the state attracts shoppers from nearby states.

TAX FREEDOM DAY 2012

Tax freedom day is the date on which earnings no longer go to taxes. It is calculated by dividing total taxes collected by total income. Selected "freedom days" are listed below.

Tennessee: March 31 (earliest in the nation)

Maine: April 8

Florida: April 12

New Hampshire: April 16

United States: April 13

Rhode Island: April 17

Connecticut: May 5 (last in the nation)

Source: Tax Foundation

Did you know. . .

. . . that Maine is the home of the Jackson Laboratory, the world's largest non-profit mammalian genetic research facility? Jackson Lab in Bar Harbor is the world's largest supplier of genetically purebred mice. It was founded by a former University of Maine president, C.C. Little.

The Great Maine Woods

The first sawmill built in Maine was built in 1634 in Berwick as early English explorers harvested trees. Maine, specifically the city of Bangor, became known as the Lumber Capital of the World. Indeed by 1830, the city had more than 300 sawmills processing logs from the northern woods.

When rivers were not frozen, logs constantly jammed them, especially the Penobscot. The white pine, scarce in Europe and ideal for shipbuilding and masts, became the state's most important export. Maine's woods provided the lumber for shipbuilding and Maine dominated that industry until the wooden schooners gave way to steamships in the 1920s. Through the 20th century, Maine continued to count forest products as its number one industry even though usage changed from masts and ships to cardboard boxes, paper bags, wood pulp, paper, and other products. Put in perspective, as late as the 1950s there were almost 2,000 wood manufacturing plants in the state.

Even the lowly toothpick earned fortunes for a few entrepreneurs who began turning them out in the late 19th century. Up to 20 billion were produced by one company in one year at the peak.

Wood in one form or another has contributed the largest share of Maine's income from manufacturing. Throughout most of the 20th century, Maine has depended more on paper and pulp as an industry. Indeed paper products as an industry continues to be a leading source of industrial production. The industry, however, is under increasing threat as mills close because of costs or foreign competition.

Still Maine continues to be the most heavily forested state in the US; about 90 percent of Maine's area is covered in forest. Paper companies continue to own or control the majority of forest lands, but now the second-largest owner of woodlands is Roxanne Quimby, multimillionaire cofounder of Burt's Bees, a line of natural cosmetics and body care products. Some of the 70,000 acres of land owned by her Elliotsville Plantation, Inc. foundation, abuts Baxter State Park.

The industry is in a state of change. The University of Maine's Advanced Engineered Wood Composite (AEWC) Center was established to explore innovative ways to strengthen wood and by so doing for new uses and new markets for wood. The center has been enormously successful and it is estimated more than 200 products have been developed or enhanced since the center opened.

INCOME

Maine's per capita personal income was $33,481 in 2012. This amount is lower than the US average of $42,693. Selected state figures:

West Virginia 34,477
Alabama 35,625
Iowa 42,126
Vermont 42,994
California 44,980
Massachusetts 54,687

Source: US Bureau Economic Analysis

FAMILY INCOME

According to the US Census Bureau, Maine's median family income for the years 2006-2007 averaged $47,415, placing it at 32 in the ranking of states, behind its New England neighbors. New Hampshire was number one with $66,652, while Connecticut came in 4th with $64,158, Massachusetts was 10th with $57,681, Rhode Island was 14th with $54,735 and Vermont was 19th with $50,423.

MAINE MINIMUM WAGE

At least 20,000 Mainers worked in full-time or part-time jobs earning the state minimum, according to Department of Labor statistics. Most minimum wage earners work in food preparation jobs or the lodging industry.

New Hampshire has the lowest minimum wage in New England at $7.25 an hour. Maine is $7.50 an hour and Rhode Island is $7.40 an hour. Connecticut, Massachusetts, and Vermont are $8.00 an hour.

Maine's first minimum wage – in 1959 – was $1.00 an hour.

GENDER (IM)BALANCE

Women's median earnings in Maine are 77.0 percent those of men. The figure for the US as a whole was 77.5 percent. Among the New England states, Vermont had the greatest parity with women earning 84.1 percent of men's wages, while New Hampshire had the least with women taking home 69.5 percent of men's earnings.

Source: Maine Department of Labor

Tourism

Tourism has grown to be the second largest industry in the state (behind healthcare), accounting for 15 percent of the Gross State Product. Put in perspective, the tourism industry in tourism-driven Florida accounts for just 13 percent of its Gross State Product.

As much as the state likes to tout its urban draws, the tourists come for the untouched beauty and the Maine lifestyle. In an increasingly urban America, Maine values of neighborliness and rugged independence are qualities disappearing from the American landscape.

Tourists to Maine take 10 million overnight trips every year and more than 30 million day trips. Travelers spent nearly $1 billion on lodging, $3 billion on food, and $1 billion on recreational activities. More than 70,000 jobs depend on tourism.

The State Planning Office found that the economic impact of tourism in Maine is such that it generates $10 billion in sales of goods and services. The latest figures show tourism accounts for almost $550 million in state and local taxes.

The energy generated by tourism is akin to seeing gardens grow. Summer sees the population of small, quiet towns expand, sometimes by ten fold. Many Mainers have strong friendships with regular summer visitors.

The mystique that attaches to Maine is used by the purveyors of everything from soap to food products who use the state's name to appeal to those who hold "Vacationland" in a special place in their hearts. Mainers' hustle and ingenuity has once again taken what nature has thrown at them and turned it into a viable enterprise.

EMPLOYMENT BY SECTOR

Service industry	38 percent
Transportation, public utilities	21 percent
Wholesale, retail trade	21 percent
Government	17 percent
Finance, insurance, real estate	14 percent
Manufacturing	9 percent
Construction	5 percent
Farming, forestry, fishing	2 percent

Boom Years

The period between 1820 and 1860 were truly the boom years, something Maine had not experienced before or since. The population literally doubled. More than 9,000 ships were built at Maine shipyards during this period and more than 20 percent of the country's merchant marine was owned by Maine. The value of Maine's fish catch was second in the nation and the state led the nation in the number of registered fishing vessels. Agriculture and textile, lime and granite production also achieved rapid growth during this period.

Past and Future

Founded in 1962, Fairchild Semiconductor's South Portland plant is the longest continuously operating semiconductor manufacturing facility in the world, and Fairchild is the largest publicly traded company headquartered in Maine. The Portland facility employs approximately 850 workers and the site also serves as one of the corporate offices for Fairchild.

As the leading global supplier of high performance semiconductors, the site develops and manufactures chips, or integrated circuits, used in everything from computing, communications, industrial, automotive, and consumer applications. Fairchild develops many leading products right here in Maine. They have customers worldwide; however a majority is located in Asia, accounting for nearly 80 percent of their total market.

"Although it is less common now, we still have workers that have been employed at Fairchild for over 40 years," says Patti Olson, Fairchild's Corporate Communications manager. "We've stayed in Maine because of the stability of the workforce. The people here want to be in Maine," she says. "Fairchild is also able to utilize local educational resources. For instance, the company partners with the universities and employs summer co-ops. This provides a vital learning experience for the students, and some of them go on to become employees, in engineering, finance, or other areas."

Portland also provides a transportation hub for the company. The airport allows the company to ship products out of Maine to other Fairchild locations in the United States and Asia. Fairchild continues to see Maine as part of its future, and for the state of Maine it provides a crucial link in the jobs and industry of tomorrow.

Fairchild is a $1.4 billion company, publicly traded on the NYSE, with over 50,000 customers worldwide and listed as one of the top 30 semiconductor companies in the world. Today, Fairchild is a global leader delivering energy-efficient analog, discrete, signal path, and optoelectronic solutions. Their focus is on the design and development of products that increase energy efficiency and connect people to electronic appliances.

HOUSE COSTS BY COUNTY

Average listing price for homes.

County	Price
Hancock	$470,757
Lincoln	$420,723
Knox	$398,422
York	$393,339
Cumberland	$370,343
Washington	$336,231
Sagadahoc	$291,826
Franklin	$286,172
Waldo	$286,113
Oxford	$224,666
Kennebec	$213,635
Piscataquis	$196,683
Penobscot	$195,996
Androscoggin	$188,606
Somerset	$178,712
Aroostook	$143,937

Did you know. . .

. . . that compared to other states, Maine has the highest concentration (seventeen times the national average) of leather manufacturing jobs in the country?

Did you know. . .

. . . that are no Mainers on Forbes' 2008 list of the 400 Richest Americans?

They said it

"*The Creative Economy is a catalyst for the creation of new jobs in Maine communities. People who create jobs want to live in places that have a diverse cultural mix and an innovative and educated workforce. Maine will be competitive economically if we continue to capitalize on the synergies between entrepreneurship, education, the arts and quality of life.*"

– Governor John Elias Baldacci

SMALL BUSINESS

- Number of small business (those businesses with fewer than 500 employees) in Maine: 149,644
- Of those, the number that had more than one employee: 34,771
- Number of large employers with greater than 500 employees: 916
- Percentage of state employers accounted for by Maine small business: 97.4
- Percentage of private sector employment accounted for by small business: 60.6

Source: Small Business Administration

GOVERNMENT JOBS

Seventeen percent of those employed in Maine work for the federal, state, and municipal governments.

- Federal: 14,400 employees
- State: 28,000 employees
- Municipal: 60,100 employees

Source: Maine Labor Market Digest, February 2009.

Did you know. . .

. . . that Maine added personal and corporate income taxes in 1969?

TRANSPORTATION INFRASTRUCTURE

Road: Maine is a state that relies mostly on its road systems for transportation of passengers, goods, and services. There are 22,792 miles of highways; 367 of those miles are part of the federal interstate highway system. Interstate 95 is the main route and links most of the state's bigger cities. There are currently two main trunk lines, American Realty and the Golden Road, which run between Ashland and Daaquam, Quebec, and between Millinocket and Saint Zacharie, Quebec, that are the most important two roads in the northern part of the state.

Rail: Like in many areas, rail service has been gradually declining in Maine, and currently only regional and local railroads are serving the state. There are 1,148 miles of tracks that carry goods originating from Maine. Around 60 percent of the tonnage exported through rail is pulp and paper, and about 23 percent is wood products and lumber. The freight service is provided by Pan Am Railways; St. Lawrence and Atlantic Railroad; Maine Eastern Railroad; Montreal, Maine, and Atlantic Railway; and New Brunswick Southern Railway.

Air: Maine has six airports, the two largest being Portland International Jetport and Bangor International Airport. Daily service connects Maine's largest cities to Boston, Orlando, and New York City, along with several other national localities. The four smaller airports are served by 19- to 30-seat planes courtesy of US Airways Express.

Did you know. . .

. . . that the Stanley Brothers of Kingfield, who invented the Stanley Steamer automobile, were 6-foot-tall identical twins who whittled their first violins at age 10 and taught themselves to play? They manufactured the Stanley violin before switching to mass-producing the first successful dry photographic plate. After selling out to George Eastman of Eastman-Kodak, they turned their steam car hobby into a successful commercial venture.

Port: The Port of Portland is the largest tonnage seaport in New England. In 2007 it processed some 149,616,287 barrels of oil, making it the second largest oil port on the east coast, and the largest foreign inbound transit tonnage port in the United States. Portland is also the second largest port of call in Maine for cruise ships after Bar Harbor.

Marden's and Reny's

Marden's Surplus & Salvage and R.H. Reny, Inc., or Marden's and Reny's (or Chez Reny), to Mainers, seem unconcerned with the long march of Wal-Mart and the Big Box stores. They are virtually state institutions now. Reny's logo shows the name Reny's against a background of pine trees with the words "A Maine Adventure" underneath. They're the kind of stores people rush home to call their friends to inform them about the latest good deal.

Harold "Call me Mickey" Marden's two-pronged philosophy when he launched his first tiny store in Fairfield in 1964 was, "Don't buy anything you have to feed" and "There is a buyer for anything at the right price." He seems to have been right.

Mickey died in 2002, but three of his children (Harold, David, and Nancy) carry on the multi-million dollar business with several hundred employees. The first store was about the size of the average shoe section in one of Marden's 14 stores that dot the state. There are even plans to expand.

Robert "R.H." Reny started his first store in 1949 in Damariscotta. To keep the store afloat the first winter, he went door-to-door selling merchandise from his old Hudson. From socks to TVs, Reny's sells darn near anything. With 14 stores throughout the state, the company employs up to 475 people. Both chains buy brand-name closeouts, salvage, and other bargain lots, and both are renowned for their old-fashioned way of doing business.

EXPORTS

International trade supports 1,707 companies and creates 143,000 jobs in Maine.

- Total exports 2008: $3,011,497,297
- Total today: 3,164,991,540
- Change: – 24.54 percent

Source: Maine International Trade Center, Census Bureau

COMMERCIAL FISHING LANDINGS

Maine's fishing industry is the historic mainstay of many coastal communities. Total value caught in 2012 was $435,030,033.

- American lobster   77 percent
- Atlantic salmon   6 percent
- Soft clam   3 percent
- Groundfish   3 percent
- Atlantic herring   2 percent
- Worms   2 percent
- Green sea urchin   1 percent
- Mahogany quahog   1 percent
- Northern shrimp   1 percent
- Goosefish   1 percent
- Other fish   3 percent

TAKE5 TOP FIVE EXPORTS
BY PRODUCT

1. **Computer and electronic products**
2. **Paper**
3. **Transportation equipment**
4. **Fish, fresh, chilled, or frozen and other marine products**
5. **Forestry products**

Source: Maine International Trade Center

Maine is the largest supplier of lobster in the country with annual landings in excess of 63,000,000 lbs. valued at well over $320 million. The historic high was 2006, with landings of 75,298,119 lbs., valued at $311.7 million. In 2008, the industry hit a major hurdle—high fuel prices coincided with a downturn in demand and low prices for lobsters; sometimes as low as $2/lb.

Source: Maine Department of Marine Resources and NOAA Fisheries

Did you know. . .

. . . that a Maine lawmaker submitted a bill in 2009 to allow employees to ask colleagues how much they earn, without having to fear retribution from the boss? The bill, aimed at shrinking the male-female wage gap, was amended by a legislative committee to say that employees could ask, but that their colleagues didn't have to answer.

Did you know. . .

. . . that textile mills first migrated from Massachusetts to Maine in the early 19th century? Mills were established along the state's rivers, fueled by hydro-power and labor from surrounding farming communities.

TAKE 5 TOP FIVE COUNTIES IN AGRICULTURE SALES, PERCENTAGE OF STATE TOTAL RECEIPTS

1. **Aroostook:** 26.1 percent
2. **Androscoggin:** 20.8 percent
3. **Washington:** 8.9 percent
4. **Kennebec:** 6.5 percent
5. **Penobscot:** 6.2 percent

Source: Maine Department of Agriculture

AGRICULTURE

Much of Maine's soil is rocky and despite vast tracts of land, only three percent of Maine's land is used to grow crops. Many of the farms are sidelines for operators who also have jobs off the farm. Still agriculture as an industry is important to Maine.

Including potatoes and all other crops, Maine's farms produced a market value of more than $450 million. Adding associated industries, such as processors, suppliers, and retailers, agriculture contributes about $1.2 billion to Maine's economy and employs more than 65,000 workers.

Potatoes and blueberries are the most well known crops of Maine agriculture, but crops such as ornamentals—trees, shrubs, and flowers— grown on much smaller farms have a very high value, generating over $300 million annually. Even those classified as fruits and vegetable farms, many under 20 acres (often near high population areas), contribute $30 million dollars in sales annually. Forage crops, such as hay, silage, and grain, are also vital to the state's agricultural mix.

POTATOES

Potatoes have been the mainstay of Maine's and Aroostook County's economy for more than 200 years. In 2001, the humble Maine potato neared the economic value of the more upscale Maine lobster when sales of potatoes passed $125 million while lobster landings were valued at $153 million.

Aroostook County is the leading potato-producing region of Maine, and almost all potato production in the county happens in an area about 30 miles wide and 100 miles long.

The impact of the potato industry on Maine's economy today is $540 million in sales, 6,100 jobs, more than $230 million in personal income, and more than $32 million in state and local taxes.

Organic Maine

The oldest and largest state organic organization in the country is the Maine Organic Farmers and Gardeners Association (MOFGA). Established in 1971 during a nationwide "return to the earth" movement, MOFGA has grown from a tiny group of hippies to an organization with 18 employees and more than 5,000 members.

Organic farming principles have caught on, too. In 1995, Aroostook organic farmer James Cook decided the increasing number of organic growers needed a reliable distribution system.

He launched Crown O'Maine Cooperative (COMOC), distributing produce from his own Skylandia Organic Farm in Grand Isle, and that of any interested farmer. Cook, known as the face of organic farming in Maine, died in 2008, but his family continues the work.

Crown O'Maine has grown to include distribution of many gourmet specialty items created by Maine's small food producers who are not farmers.

In recent years, consumers concerned about the safety of their food, as well as its "carbon footprint," have signed on to a new concept: Community Supported Agriculture (CSAs) and Community Supported Fisheries (CSFs).

Memberships in CSAs have taken off in a few short years, with more than 120 farms, mostly organic, participating in the program and more than 5,500 shares sold. Subscribers sign on for a season's share in the produce from a farm, choosing the size of their share depending on the weekly amount of vegetables they want.

CSFs operate the same way. Consumers buy shares of shrimp in season, or whichever fish is landed, at a fair price, and the fishermen receive a better price for their catch by eliminating the middleman.

TAKE 5 FIVE OFFBEAT MAINE
COMMERCIAL SEAFOOD PRODUCTS

1. **Periwinkle**
2. **Sandworm**
3. **Sea Cucumber**
4. **Seaweed**
5. **Bloodworm**

BLUEBERRIES

Maine is the largest producer of wild blueberries in the world. It accounts for 15 percent of the North American blueberry crop, which includes the cultivated high-bush berries. Maine's 60,000 acres of wild blueberries produce more than 70 million pounds annually, with only half of them in production each year. Less than 1 percent of the crop is sold fresh, while 99 percent are frozen. Organic blueberries, which sell for more money, are now grown on 854 acres, or 1.4 percent of Maine's blueberry barrens.

Sources: University of Maine Cooperative Extension; US Department of Agriculture and Maine Department of Agriculture

MAINE FARMS

- Total number of farms: 7,196
- Total farmland acreage: 19,750,000 acres
- Average farm size: 190 acres
- Average age of farm operators: 53.7 years
- Farmers who are men: 5,637
- Farmers who are women: 1,559

Source: Government of Maine

Weblinks

Maine Department of Agriculture

www.maine.gov/agriculture

A site designed to educate the public on the state's agriculture, to promote its natural resources, and to ensure a safe, wholesome, high quality food supply.

Maine Made

www.mainemade.com

Selected products from furniture to food that reflect fine Maine craftsmanship.

Made In Maine

www.madeinmaine.com

A range of some signature Maine products selected for your consideration.

Did you know. . .

. . . that from 2005 to 2008, organic milk production was the fastest-growing area in Maine's agricultural sector with 72 farms? The economic downturn caused large milk buyers to cut production in early 2009.

Did you know. . .

. . . that Maine has the fifth fairest state tax system in the nation, according to the Washington-based Corporation for Enterprise Development, and the most favorable overall tax environment in New England, according to a CFO Magazine State Tax Survey? Maine also offers exceptional Tax Reimbursement programs for qualified businesses.

Then and Now

MAINE AS A PERCENTAGE OF US POPULATION
1900: 0.9 percent
1950: 0.6 percent
2013: 0.4 percent

MAINE'S POPULATION HISTORY
1790	96,540
1810	228,705
1850	583,169
1890	661,086
1910	742,371
1950	913,774
1990	1,227,928
2015	1,329,328

BIRTH RATE, PER 1,000 POPULATION
	Maine	US
1900	20.3	30.0
1947	26.7	26.6
1990	14.1	16.7
2013	10.5	14.4

Source: US Census

INFANT MORTALITY

More than 25 percent of infants born in Maine in 1900 died. Today the infant mortality rate has decreased to 0.5 percent.

POVERTY

Some 24 percent of Mainers lived below the national poverty line in 1960. That number had decreased to 11.5 percent. Fifty-six percent of Maine's poor and 60 percent of the unemployed currently live in rural areas, with rural per capita income 24 percent lower than that of urban dwellers.

Source: Changing Maine

EDUCATION

Maine decided to help pay to educate its children in 1828 but didn't make school attendance compulsory until 1875, and as a result schools were poorly attended well into the late 18th and early 19th centuries. They were often run by poorly trained teachers and located haphazardly. In one instance, in Kennebunk, residents converted a fish house into a school.

Towns funded their own schools and often parents had to buy shares in order to send their older children on to 'grammar' schools. Only seven Maine towns had grammar schools in 1800, but all 161 towns had 'common' schools for younger children. In 1821 Portland was the first community in Maine, and the second in the nation, to open a free high school.

Maine now has 286 school districts serving around 280,000 K-8 students, only 730 students per district. In 1960, Maine spent $300 per student and provided one teacher for every 24 students. Today the price per student had risen to $8,000 but the student-teacher ratio is one to 14.

Did you know. . .

. . . that no fewer than seven cow-tail holder patents were applied for by Maine inventors?

ALL THE LIVE LONG DAY

- Year in which trains first traversed the state: 1836, between Old Town and Bangor
- Year of the first passenger train: 1842
- Time it takes the Amtrak Downeaster to travel between Boston and Portland in 2007: Two hours
- Time it took to get from Boston to Portland on the "Flying Yankee" train on the Maine Central Railroad in 1935: 1 hour, 9 minutes (51 minutes faster than the Downeaster).
- Number of passengers to ride on Maine's railway system in 1920: 4 million
- Number of passengers in 1933: 375,000
- Number of passengers in 2006: 329,365
- Total length of all tracks in the rail system at its peak in 1924: 2,380 miles
- Total length of all tracks in Maine's rail system today: 1,148 miles
- Last year of operation of passenger trains offering service between Boston and Portland before the return of service in 2001: 1965

Source: Maine: The Pine Tree State from Prehistory to Present, Maine.gov.

AUTOMOBILES

- Year in which the "King's Highway" was built, creating the road between Kittery and Portland that would later become Route 1: 1653
- Number of days it took to travel from Portland to Portsmouth by stagecoach in 1787: 3
- Year in which the Maine Turnpike opened to traffic between Portland and Portsmouth: 1947
- Number of miles of all roads in Maine in 1905: 25,530
- Number of miles of public roads today: 22,792
- Number of miles of public roads that are unpaved: 4,000
- Number of registered motor vehicles in 1905 (the year after the Motor Vehicle Division of state government was created by the State Legislature): 715

- Number of registered motor vehicles in Maine in 1915: 24,472
- Number of registered motor vehicles in Maine: 1,491,149

FEWER COWS TO TIP

In 60 years, Maine lost 93 percent of its dairy farms; yet even today dairy farms still employ more than 1,200 people full time and indirectly support another 1,500 while delivering $100 million to the state's economy.

1940: 5,000+ dairy farms

1986: 775

2013: Less than 400

AGRICULTURE: UP & DOWN

When Maine became a state in 1820, there were 55,031 farmers tilling 78,964 acres of land. Maine's agricultural economy continued to grow with larger farms and more diversified crops. Farms began to rely on producing items like barrels, boots, and straw hats to sell at local markets.

Today's most productive crops include forage crops such as hay and grass silage at 209,955 acres, potatoes at 64,474 acres, barley at 25,856 acres, oats at 24,919 acres, and corn for silage at 24,351 acres.

Although small farms declined in Maine in recent decades, Mainers are beginning to increase the number of acres tilled as they move into production of organic crops.

THE BRITISH ARE COMING – FOR THE TREES

In 1691, after hearing reports of the vast forests of Maine, the British crown established the Broad Arrow Policy, requiring that any white pine tree more than 23 inches in diameter and within three miles of the coastline be marked with the point of a broad arrow, reserved to be used as masts for the Royal Navy. The white pine is still sometimes referred to in Maine as the King's Pine. Now the pine trees are harvested mainly for pulp and lumber.

TAKE **5** FIVE MAJOR MAINE
SHIPWRECKS

1. **The passenger steamer *Portland*** went down in a November 1898 storm, appropriately called the Portland Gale, while making her regular run from Boston to Portland. All passengers and crew, estimated at around 190, were lost in the area of Stellwagen Bank in the Gulf of Maine. It is considered the worst maritime disaster in New England's history.

2. **The passenger steamer *Royal Tar*** was destroyed by fire in October 1836 in Penobscot Bay, on a regular run from St. John, NB to Portland. The boiler ran dry and ignited the ship's wooden structure. Many were saved, but 28 passengers and four crew died, along with the performers in a wild animal show traveling on the steamer; two lions, six horses, two dromedaries, an elephant, a leopard, a Bengal tiger, a gnu, two pelicans, and a collection of snakes.

3. **The sailing vessel *Nottingham Galley*** was wrecked on a voyage from London to Boston at Boon Island in December 1710. The entire 14-man crew survived the wreck, but that number was reduced to 12 after two men died of exposure. The last man was eaten for food.

4. **The ship *Grand Design*** carrying Scots-Irish immigrants wrecked around 1739, at an unidentified island or neck of land on the coast of Maine. Abandoned by captain and crew, about 100 survivors of the wreck were left to fend for themselves for more than two months in late fall. Most died of starvation or disappeared in the forest.

5. **The ship *Hanover*** was wrecked at Popham Beach, returning with Spanish salt to her home port of Bath in November 1849. Practically within her home river, in full daylight while people watched from the beach, she caught on a sand bar and was destroyed by storm-heightened seas. No one survived.

TOOTHPICK CAPITAL OF THE WORLD

Benjamin Franklin Sturtevant of Norridgewock developed the technology to make toothpicks about 150 years ago and ran the Maine mills that turned them out by the trainload. Businessman Charles Forster, a Buckfield native, made Strong, Maine, the largest toothpick center in the world. He owned the plants that turned out 200 million wooden toothpicks a day, using methods that changed little for a century and a half.

The process involved steaming birch logs and 'unrolling' them to cut flat toothpicks out of the thin sheets of wood. Round toothpicks were made by cutting oversized slivers of the wood and inserting them in a machine to round them off. Maine manufactured 90 percent of the country's toothpicks well into the mid-20th century when the industry was forced out by lower-cost foreign production.

PACKING 'EM IN, NO MORE

Maine's sardine canning industry was once the largest in the nation, earning $40 million annually and producing 75 million cans of sardines in 418 canneries at its peak. The industry's name was always a misnomer, because the fish canned were actually herring, not the tiny sardines found in Pacific waters.

Herring packed here were larger and required cutting the heads and tails off with razor-sharp scissors. No job for the squeamish – or the slow – since packers were paid per can.

The industry peaked in the 1950s, when the cans held the first "fast" food. Returning war veterans could bring sardines to work in their lunch pails without worrying about refrigeration.

The industry died out near the end of the 20th century. The number of

Did you know. . .

. . . that Portland was a major maritime port in the 19th century because it was one day closer to England than Boston was? It also served as Canada's winter port.

plants plummeted, leaving the coast of downeast Maine with boarded-up canneries and unemployed workers. Maine herring landings peaked in 1968 with 469,000 tons. The fishery suffered a severe collapse during the seventies, and 1994 brought a record low catch of 76,000 tons. Now, only one plant survives, but the industry's history is preserved in a new museum – the Maine Coast Sardine History Museum in Jonesport.

From Frankenstein to Stacey

For three decades, Maine viewers were treated to what might have been the first reality show. Except this one was really real.

It all began in the late 1950s when Bob Whitten launched "Frankenstein's Country Jamboree" from Milbridge on NBC affiliate, WLBZ-TV in Bangor. Amateur singers lined up to appear on the show that had no rehearsals or auditions.

Talent was not a requirement. Ads for "the Frankensteins," as the show was popularly known, were replete with illustrations of the monster-scars, bolts and all. One stationary camera meant viewers watched performers walk to and from the mike.

In 1972, Dick Stacey, Bangor gas station owner, took over sponsorship of the show, renaming it "Stacey's Country Jamboree." Dick did his own commercials, always using the line, "See these hands, they pump gas, and they stink."

Everything about the show was down-home. A little old lady from Bucksport named Jenny Shontell appeared regularly, usually singing "Wings of a Dove" – always off-key. She was so bad she had a following. At least once per show, a guitar-strummer in a fancy Western shirt would sing "Haynesville Woods," the trucking song written by Maine's Dick Curless.

Stacey had agreed to sponsor the show for a maximum of 13 weeks, but that stretched into 11 years. The show went off the air in 1983 when Maritime cable companies opted for feeds from Detroit rather than Bangor.

TAKE 5 RENNY STACKPOLE'S FIVE
REASONS MAINE'S MARITIME HISTORY IS UNIQUE

Renny Stackpole, historian, is the former director of the Penobscot Marine Museum and serves on the Maine State Museum Commission. He lives in his ancestral home in Thomaston.

1. **Geography:** Maine has a coastline containing over 5,300 miles of bays, rivers, and islands. Known simply as "the Main" by early explorers, by 1600, Basques, French, and English mariners had set up fishing stations on remote islands like Damariscove and Monhegan. By the turn of the 18th century, coastal settlements were established and a distinct maritime culture developed around fishing, boatbuilding, and trading. Great proprietors like Samuel Waldo later recruited artisans from Scotland, Ireland, and Wales to settle along the rivers and streams, as great tracts of land were sought for the crown in order to supply the Royal Navy with tall pines for ship's masts. Following the American Revolution, thousands of veterans flocked to Maine seeking cheap land for homesteading.

2. **Shipbuilding:** With the advent of water-powered machinery for cutting timber, Maine's fast flowing rivers and streams were used to produce ships, large and small. Towns like Thomaston, Bath, Waldoboro, Kittery, and Belfast became centers for ship construction. Ships were built in a prudent fashion as the merchants of each town invested in each ship in multiples of eight, thus spreading the risk of ownership or insurance. The term "when my ship comes in" had significant reason for Maine folk who could invest in voyages. Driving through these towns today, one can appreciate the lovely homes built by families that made a fortune in ship construction. By 1870 the little town of Thomaston boasted four millionaires among the 3,500 residents.

3. **A Nursery of Seamen and Shipmasters:** Certain Maine towns became famous for producing shipmasters and Searsport headed the list by the 1880s when 10 percent of all American shipmasters in the "deepwater sailing trade" came from the town on the

northern shore of Penobscot Bay. The Penobscot Marine Museum in Searsport has preserved the center of the village with historic buildings full of ship models and portraits. Bath's Maine Maritime Museum also boasts both a maritime history building and the site of the Percy and Small Shipyard, where hundreds of schooners were built for the carrying trade for coal and case oil during the 19th and early 20th centuries. One of Maine's great ships, the *St. Mary*, was wrecked in the Falkland Island on its maiden voyage. Marine archaeologists from Maine returned the timbers to the Maine State Museum in Augusta, where a visitor can appreciate the massive timbers required in the great ships of that time.

4. **Letters from Sea:** Letter writing was sometimes the only means of communication for seafaring families. The Libraries of the Penobscot Marine Museum and Maine Maritime Museum contain a vibrant archive of letters and log books for the public to peruse. One collection in Searsport offers a glimpse into the lives of the Lincoln Alden Colcord family. The daughter Joanna sailed with her parents on many voyages from New York to Hong Kong and was home-schooled while living aboard the vessels *Harvard* and *State of Maine*. She completed her high school final exams and then attended the University of Maine with her younger brother, Lincoln, who was born in a gale off Cape Horn in the 1880s. Both became well-known writers.

5. **Maine Lighthouses:** Sixty-eight light stations were established from 1790 until the early 20th century. Hundreds of Maine families sacrificed creature comforts to man the lights in all seasons of the year. A visit to the Maine Lighthouse Museum in Rockland provides the visitor with a glimpse of the mechanisms that made lighthouse keeping so exacting. Here the stories are told of heroines like young Abbie Burgess who was required to keep the twin lights at Matinicus Rock burning for a long week amid winter gales while her father was stranded on the mainland and her mother was ill in bed. The Coast Guard cutter *Abbie Burgess* plies both Penobscot Bay and River in all seasons of the year to keep her spirit of service alive.

They said it

MAINE MEDAL OF HONOR WINNERS

The US Congressional Medal of Honor was established by Congress eight months into the Civil War, on December 21, 1861. Since then, 76 Mainers have earned the country's highest distinction for "conspicuous gallantry... above and beyond the call of duty."

The first was Joshua L. Chamberlain, Maine's most famous Civil War hero. Another was war hero Air Force Major Charles Loring Jr. of Portland, who fought in Korea, and for whom Loring Air Force Base in Limestone was named. A 3' by 4' bronze plaque bearing all 76 names and the wars and campaigns in which they served is displayed in the state capitol's Hall of Flags.

Did you know. . .

. . . that the Rockland windjammer, *Stephen Taber*, is the oldest documented sailing vessel in continuous service in the US? The 68' schooner was built as a coasting schooner in 1871 on Long Island, New York and was recently designated as a National Historic Landmark.

CIVIL WAR

Experts say between 618,000 and 700,000 Americans died in the Civil War, a number that exceeds the nation's loss in all other wars combined, from the Revolution through Vietnam.

TAKE5 ROSEY GERRY'S FIVE SIGNS
OF AN OLD, ABANDONED ROAD

Rosey Gerry has worked in the woods all his life, where he can't resist following and uncovering the location of old Maine roads when he sees signs. He's documented three, gives talks on the subject, and has led hikes to publicize them. One two-day hike took 33 people across the old road from Ducktrap in Lincolnville to Augusta.

1. **Old dig-outs by the sides of what were once old roads**. These were the excavations made to get materials to make the road.

2. **Old stone culverts made of flat rocks**. They're usually not in good shape, but if you see piles of flat rocks in a depression, they're often old culverts.

3. **Stone walls in the middle of nowhere**. Camden Hills State Park is covered in stone walls in the woods. How did they get there? Aliens didn't bring them. Stone walls mean people lived there and they had to have a road.

4. **Small conifers growing in the middle, but ruts or beaten-down areas along the side**. They're easiest to see in winter with about two to three inches of snow; it hollows them out.

5. **The straightness**. Most of the old roads started as Indian trails and they were efficient. Unless they had to go around a mountain, a lake or another natural impediment, the roads are perfectly straight. And the Indians had no compasses. The other settlers had no power tools or chain saws. All these roads were cut by hand.

TAKE 5 FIVE MAINE INVENTIONS

1. **Donut hole machine**
2. **Earmuffs**
3. **Motor ice boat** (a forerunner of the snowmobile)
4. **Toothpick**
5. **Thermostat**

One regiment, the 1st Maine Heavy Artillery, in a charge at Petersburg, Virginia, on June 18, 1864, sustained a "record" loss of the war – 635 of its 900 men within seven minutes. In the space of 10 months 66.5 percent of the unit was lost.

In his book *Civil War Regiments from Maine, 1861-1865*, Bowdoin college professor Joshua Lawrence Chamberlain wrote that Maine soldiers suffered an 18.9 percent casualty rate, the highest percentage of loss for any Union state during the war.

Chamberlain, wounded six times in the war, served with the Twentieth Maine Infantry that helped defend Little Round Top during the battle of Gettysburg, vital to the war's outcome. He rose from Lieutenant Colonel to Colonel, Brigadier General and Brevet Major General and received the first Confederate surrenders at Appomattox Court House, and later served as state governor and president of Bowdoin.

Did you know. . .

. . . that the man credited with launching the board game industry in North America was born in Vienna, Maine? Milton Bradley started his company of the same name when he debuted *The Checkered Game of Life* in 1860. The first run of several hundred sold out in two days, and another 40,000 were sold in the first year. Later, it was called *The Game of Life*. Bradley also invented the paper cutter.

TAKE5 WHAT THE TOP FIVE MAINE
OFFICIALS EARNED IN 1899

1. **Governor Llewellyn Powers** received a princely $2,000
2. **Secretary of State Byron Boyd** made $1,500
3. **Treasurer F. M. Simpson** earned $2,000
4. **Attorney General W. T. Haines** only brought home $1,000 (Maybe they didn't like lawyers?)
5. **Adjutant General John T. Richards** pocketed a bit more, at $1,500

WORLD WAR II

When the US entered World War II, Maine's population represented 0.63 of the country's population, but the state managed to contribute 0.62 percent of the men and women to the army. Of those who left, 3.61 percent of them failed to return. Mainers comprised of 0.7 percent of the army's dead and missing. Maine suffered a total of 2,165 casualties.

1930 COSTS

The average price of a home in 1930 was $7,145. Today, the median price of a home in the Portland area had dropped to $150,000. In 1930, a gallon of gas cost 10 cents. After hitting a high of well above $4 in 2008, they were back to $3.68 in 2013. The car to put the gas in cost about $745 in 1930, but today averages about $25,000. An average salary in 1930 was $1,970, while Maine's median annual salary for an individual today is $24,977. A loaf of bread cost 9 cents, but today it's closer to $3 or $5 for an organic artisan loaf.

Did you know. . .

. . . that Togus was the first Veteran's Hospital in the United States? The facility was founded in 1866 and is still in operation.

They said it

MAINE MEDIA

- Year in which Maine's first radio station, WMB, went on the air from its station in Auburn: 1922
- Number of radio stations in Maine by 1959: 30
- Year in which Mainers could first pick up television signals trailing in from stations in Providence and Boston: 1949
- Year in which the state's first TV station, WABI-TV, began broadcasting from Bangor: 1953
- Number of TV stations by 1954: 8
- Year in which the *Falmouth Gazette*, Maine's first newspaper was first printed: 1785

Did you know. . .

. . . that four US Navy ships have been named *USS Maine* in honor of the state?

Did you know. . .

. . . that Clyde Sukeforth, born in Washington, Maine, went from a 1920s semi-pro Augusta baseball team to play in the major leagues and later to become a scout and coach? He scouted and signed Jackie Robinson, the first black player in modern major league baseball.

Weblinks

Maine Memory Network
http://www.mainememory.net/
The website of Maine Historical Society's Memory Network, a digital library that collects Maine history resources; it's often billed as Maine's online museum.

Maine State Government; Facts and History
www.maine.gov/portal/facts_history
A webpage on the state government's site that lists links to various resources for information about the state.

Did you know. . .

. . . that the traditional name for a skillful competitor in the sport of birling (log-rolling) is a Bangor Tiger? This was the name given to Penobscot river-drivers in the nineteenth century.

Did you know. . .

. . . that more than 50,000 Mainers were members of the Klu Klux Klan in 1924? When Ralph Owen Brewster ran for governor in that year, his xenophobic opposition to Catholics and immigrants won him the support of the Klan, helping him win the office.

Politics

As the population of present day Maine grew after the Revolution, settlers began to increasingly resent being ruled from Boston. The small clique of powerful Massachusetts coastal merchants, of course, rejected the separation movement, but what the War of 1812 demonstrated to Mainers was that Massachusetts was unwilling to provide protection against British raids at a time when they needed it most.

This fuelled separatist sentiment, which culminated in the autumn of 1819 with delegates meeting in Portland for 21 days to develop a state constitution. The document still reflects Maine's political values today. It clearly outlines the importance of political independence, gives voice to religious freedom, and establishes popular control of government to the people.

Congress granted Maine statehood in 1820 and it entered the Union as the 23rd state. Under the Missouri Compromise, the arrangement allowed Maine to join the Union as a free state, while Missouri, entering a year later, joined as a slave state, keeping in tact the balance between the number of free and slave states.

In 1820, Maine had a population of more than 300,000. William King, a prominent Bath merchant and shipbuilder, became the state's first governor.

Portland was selected as the state capital, but this was only temporary, and in 1832 the capital was moved permanently to Augusta.

With statehood, Maine entered an era of unprecedented economic growth. Mining and manufacturing joined lumber and shipbuilding as a boom swept the state.

NATIONAL STAGE

Maine's influence on the national stage would wane considerably as the west was settled and became more populated. Three Maine politicians, however, stand out in the nineteenth century as enormously influential both here at home and on the national stage.

Hannibal Hamlin broke with the Democratic party over the slavery question, and as a result established the Republican Party in Maine. He served as the state's first GOP governor and was elected the nation's first Republican vice president under Abraham Lincoln.

Another prominent Maine politician was James G. Blaine who dominated state and national Republican politics, first as speaker of the US House of Representatives, then as a US senator, and secretary of state in three Republican administrations. He was powerful enough that he was selected as the GOP presidential candidate in 1884, losing a closely fought race to Grover Cleveland.

Thomas B. Reed served continuously in Congress through the last quarter of the 19th century. He was a three-term House speaker, and a masterful parliamentarian who became known as "Czar Reed." He literally rewrote the book on parliamentary procedure. Indeed Reed's Rules of Order are still used in the Maine Legislature.

INDEPENDENCE

As a direct result of Hamlin, the Republican party ruled Maine politics for more than a century. It wasn't until the election of Edmund Muskie as governor in 1954 that Democrats became a legitimate force in the state.

George Mitchell and Bill Cohen, a Democrat and a Republican, respectively, served in the Senate together in the '80s and '90s and set an example for bipartisanship. They even wrote a book together. Cohen served from 1979 to 1997, when he was appointed secretary of defense under President Bill Clinton—one of the few cross-party appointments in modern history. Mitchell served from 1980 to 1995 and retired as Senate Majority Leader.

Perhaps the most important political phenomenon of modern Maine is the emergence of independent voters as a dominating force. Independents outnumber both enrolled Democrats and Republicans and provide the swing vote in most elections today.

In 1974, they helped elect the nation's only independent governor, and in 1994 Mainers did it again, electing another independent governor, Angus S. King, Jr. of Brunswick.

CURRENT ADMINISTRATION
- Governor: Paul LePage
- Political party: Republican
- Re-elected: November 4, 2014
- Legislature: 127th

HOUSE OF REPRESENTATIVES
- Number of House members: 151
- Republicans: 69
- Democrats: 78
- Independents: 3
- Unenrolled: 1
- Nonvoting members representing the Penobscot Nation, the Passamaquoddy Tribe and the Houlton Band of Maliseets: 3

SENATE
- Number of senators: 35
- Republicans: 20
- Democrats: 15

Did you know. . .

. . . that there have been 74 governors have served since statehood?

They said it

REP BY POP

- Each House member represents a district containing approximately 8,443 people
- Each Senate district represents a population of approximately 35,000

TAKE5 ANDY O'BRIEN'S FIVE REASONS
IT IS ACTUALLY FUN TO BE A MAINE REP

Andy O'Brien, 30, was elected to the Maine Legislature in 2008. He points out that Maine is one of only two states that has Clean Elections, and districts don't have a lot of residents, so lawmakers can get to know constituents.

1. **The session runs from January to June.** Since it's not a year-round, full-time job, it fills in some of the gaps of Maine's patchwork employment scene.
2. **You meet interesting candidates.** Occupations of legislators or candidates include an EMT-substitute teacher-coach-Maine Guide, and a cello teacher-firefighter-carpenter-substitute teacher-musician. (I describe myself as a landscaper-residential counselor-painter-student-freelance writer.)
3. **When you drive to the Statehouse parking lot, you don't need to feel bad about your old dented car.** It fits right in. Still, when you call, state agencies listen.
4. **They give you these cool blue license plates**, so if you cut someone off on the road, they know immediately who you are.
5. **And, you get to be addressed as "The Honorable."**

WOMEN IN THE LEGISLATURE
- House: 46 women: 30 Democrats and 16 Republicans
- Senate: 8 women: 5 Democrats and 3 Republicans

A Remarkable Gift

Baxter State Park owes its existence to one of the country's most extraordinary acts of generosity and commitment.

Percival Baxter literally devoted the second half of his life to the creation of what would become known as east coast Yellowstone. Despite being the Governor of Maine and having very meaningful connections in Washington, Baxter was unable to get either legislative body to buy the land in and around Mount Katahdin. He held summits, called in favors, and still he was unable persuade the political masters. When he finally left political life at the end of the 1920s, he took matters into his own hands.

In 1930, he struck his first important land deal with the Great Northern Paper Company for almost 6,000 acres embracing the major part of Katahdin. By the time he turned 87 years old in 1962, he donated his 28th deed to the state of Maine.

The park now contains some 202,018 acres. The 314 square miles includes 47 mountain peaks, of which 18 exceed 3,000 feet. It also includes dense boreal forest and offers unspoiled habitat for wildlife, including large game animals such as moose, deer, and black bear. The park is also the terminus of the 2,200-mile Appalachian Trail. In addition to the land, Baxter left a trust fund of nearly $7 million to ensure the park would be maintained and kept forever wild.

When Baxter died in Portland in 1969, it surprised no one in Maine that he wanted his ashes scattered across the park. Today, there is a small plaque on a boulder by Katahdin Stream that Baxter was often fond of repeating:

"*Man is born to die. His works are short-lived. Buildings crumble, monuments decay, and wealth vanishes, but Katahdin in all its glory forever shall remain the mountain of the people of Maine.*"

CONSTITUTION OF MAINE

- The Maine State Constitution created Maine's government system, with three co-equal branches; the Executive, Legislative, and Judicial branches.

Mitchell File

The George Mitchell story is really the classic American story. The son of an orphan of Irish decent and Lebanese mother, the family was straight out of working class America. When his father got laid off from Central Maine Power, he got a job as a janitor at Colby College, while his mother worked at the mill.

Young George showed an enormous aptitude for reading, and thankfully when it came time to make a post-secondary choice a family friend was able to get him an interview with admissions and into Bowdoin College. To make ends meet, Mitchell worked nights at a paper mill, and somehow still managed to play basketball, and participate in the ROTC.

While he continued his education, he decided to work at Traveler's Insurance Company during the day and attend Georgetown Law School during the night. Although he finished in the top ten percent of his class, he had difficulty getting a job back in Maine because night school law graduates were not held in high regard.

Mitchell would not be denied however, and eventually he would work two years as a trial attorney for the US Department of Justice before becoming an executive assistant to Senator Edmund S. Muskie from 1962-1965. Although he won the Democratic nomination for governor in 1974, he lost in a three-way race to Independent James Longley.

In 1977 President Jimmy Carter appointed him US Attorney for Maine. Then in 1979, Mitchell was elevated to the bench of the US District Court for Maine. He didn't remain a federal judge for long because in 1980 he was appointed to serve out Ed Muskie's term in the US Senate when Muskie resigned to become Secretary of State. In 1988 he was reelected with the largest majority of any senator from

- The presiding officer of the House is the Speaker of the House, who is elected by the members of the House.
- The State of Maine has three Constitutional Officers (the Secretary of State, the State Treasurer, and the State Attorney General) and one Statutory Officer (the State Auditor).

Maine with 81 percent of the vote.

He was elected Senate Majority Leader, a position he held until 1995. For six years running, Mitchell was voted "most respected member" of the Senate by Congressional aides. He is credited with a leadership role in passing the Americans with Disabilities Act and reauthorizing the Clean Air Act. In 1994, he turned down an appointment to the US Supreme Court to continue his Senate efforts to achieve national health care.

When he left the Senate, he became special envoy for Northern Ireland, and in a little over three years he achieved what many thought was impossible when the two sides signed the Belfast Peace Agreement in 1998. He has chaired committees investigating corruption in the Olympics and steroid use in baseball. After his success in Ireland, he was invited to chair an international fact-finding committee on the Israel-Palestine issue.

Because of his mother, Mitchell identifies himself as an Arab-American, and within days after Barack Obama became president, he was appointed special envoy to the Middle East, no doubt hoping the man from Maine will achieve in the Middle East what he did between the warring factions in Northern Ireland. It has been an incredible journey for the small town boy from Maine. Mitchell's awards are too numerous to mention but include the Presidential Medal of Freedom, a Nobel Prize nomination, an honorary knighthood, the German Peace Prize, the Truman Institute Peace Prize, and the United Nations Peace Prize.

The cost of government keeps going up, so pressure on governors to bring the budget down increases. Since the '70s, budgets have continued to go up, but the percentage of growth has gone down with each of these administrations:

1. **Longley:** 10.57 percent
2. **Brennan:** 10.5 percent
3. **McKernan:** 5.92 percent
4. **King:** 5.55 percent
5. **Baldacci:** 3.03 percent

TERMS

Maine has a biennial legislative session and the legislative term of office is two years. Maine passed term limits in 1996, so lawmakers can serve only four consecutive terms in either the House or the Senate.

Maine governors are elected for four-year terms.

SALARIES

- Governor's salary: $69,992
- Average salary earned by US governors: $124,398
- Largest: California at $206,500
- Smallest: Maine at $69,992

Did you know. . .

. . . that graduates of Bowdoin College, Maine's oldest institution of higher education, have headed each branch of the US Government? Franklin Pierce was the country's 14th president; Melville Weston Fuller served as Chief Justice of the United States; Thomas Brackett Reed was Speaker of the House of Representatives, and both Wallace White Jr. and George Mitchell served as Majority Leaders of the US Senate.

LEGISLATIVE SALARIES
- $11,384 for the first Regular Session (December to June)
- $8,655 for the second Regular Session (January to April)
- Plus another $23,000 in insurance and retirement benefits, per diem expense allowances, and tax write-offs

Source: State of Maine

ELECTORAL COLLEGE
Maine has four electoral votes in the system by which the US elects presidents. Different states have different methods for choosing electors, decided by the state's legislature, and for dividing the electoral votes, but each state has a number of electors equal to the number of representatives it has in the US House of Representatives. Forty-eight states use a winner-take-all system for their electoral votes. Only Maine (since 1972) and Nebraska (since 1992) split their votes, using the Congressional District Method (aka the Maine-Nebraska Method). Maine has two representatives and two senators, giving it four electoral votes.

Did you know. . .

. . . that former Governor John Baldacci (2003-2011) came from an Italian-Lebanese family? He is first cousin to former US Senate majority leader George J. Mitchell (whose family ancestry is Irish-Lebanese) and to famed author David Baldacci.

Did you know. . .

. . . that the Blaine House, directly across the street from the Maine State House, has been the official governor's mansion since 1919? The mansion is named after James G. Blaine, was built in 1833 by Captain James Hall, and has been a National Historic Landmark since 1964.

TAKE5 FIVE MAINE WOMEN WHO HAVE
PLAYED IMPORTANT POLITICAL ROLES
ON THE NATIONAL STAGE

1. **Dorothea Dix (1802-1887)** was born in Hampden. She was a teacher, an activist social reformer for the treatment of the mentally ill, and a superintendent of Union nurses during the American Civil War. By the time she was 54, she had traveled half the US and Europe inspecting mental institutions for mistreatment of patients. In 1854, she won passage a bill that set aside 12,225,000 acres for the benefit of the insane as well as the "blind, deaf, and dumb." The bill was vetoed by President Franklin Pierce. Many hospitals throughout the country have been named for her.

2. **Frances Perkins (1880-1965)** was born Fannie Coralie Perkins but changed her name to Frances at age 25. When she married Paul Wilson in 1913, she kept her own name and went to court to defend her choice. She earned an MA from Columbia University. The Triangle Shirtwaist Fire of 1911 propelled her to work for labor laws and to improve working conditions. She became Commissioner of Labor in New York under Gov. Franklin D. Roosevelt, who would also appoint her Secretary of Labor when he became president in 1932, in the process becoming the first woman cabinet member. She served 12 years, helping to establish the Social Security program and a large number of labor reforms. Although she was born in Boston, she spent a lot of time at the family home of her parents in Newcastle and retired there. She is in the Labor Hall of Fame.

3. **Margaret Chase Smith (1897-1995)** was one of Maine's most influential politicians. Born in Skowhegan, she was the first woman in the country to be elected to both the US House of Representatives as well as the US Senate. Her first House term was to fill the unexpired

term of her husband who passed away in office. The longest-serving woman in the Senate, she was the first person to stand up to Senator Joseph McCarthy and his Communist witch hunt, making her "Declaration of Conscience" speech on the Senate floor in 1950. In her speech, she asked her Republican Party to reject the "ride to political victory on the Four Horsemen of Calumny—Fear, Ignorance, Bigotry, and Smear." She was famous for always wearing a red rose.

4. **Olympia Jean Snowe (1947-)**, the Republican senior US Senator from Maine, was rated one of America's Top Ten Senators by Time Magazine in 2006, and is widely regarded as a moderate who can influence the outcome of filibusters and close votes. When her husband, Republican state legislator Peter Snowe, died, she ran for and won his seat, then ran for Congress at age 26, the youngest Republican woman ever elected to the House. In 1989, she married Republican Governor John McKernan, who had served in the House with her. She has never lost an election in 35 years and is considered a possible presidential candidate.

5. **Susan Collins (1952-)** was first elected to the US Senate in 1996. A Republican, she is considered a moderate. She and Snowe have been called RINOs by right-wing Republicans, or "Republicans in Name Only." They often work together to bring compromise between the parties, and both voted to acquit Bill Clinton during his impeachment hearings. Collins worked for 12 years on the staff of former Senator William Cohen, then as a finance commissioner for Governor John McKernan. She later replaced Cohen when he retired from the Senate.

VOTER TURNOUT

Maine always has a high voter turnout, attributed to the ease of registering and the availability of absentee and early voting. Maine was second in the country in 2008, with 734,000 voters participating in the presidential election.

Year	Percentage Voting in the Presidential Election
2008	70.2
2004	72.0
2000	69.2
1996	67.7
1992	74.1

Source: US Census Bureau

HOW THE GOVERNMENT GETS ITS MONEY

- Sales and Use Tax: 33 percent
- Service Provider Tax: 2 percent
- Individual Income Tax: 45 percent
- Corporate Income Tax: 6 percent
- Cigarette & Tobacco Tax: 5 percent
- Public Utilities Tax: 1 percent
- Insurance Company Tax: 2 percent
- Inheritance & Estate Tax: 1 percent
- Property Tax – Unorganized Terr.: Less than 1 percent
- Income from Investments: Less than 1 percent
- Municipal Revenue Sharing: 4 percent
- Transfer from Lottery: 2 percent
- Other Revenues: 7 percent
- TOTAL: $2,961,821,437

Source: Government of Maine

Did you know. . .

. . . that in Maine the governor hasn't had a raise in salary since 1987 and earns the lowest salary of any governor in the U.S?

TAKE**5** SUSAN W. LONGLEY'S FIVE FAVORITE
THINGS ABOUT BEING IN POLITICS IN MAINE

Susan Longley served three terms in the Maine Senate. A lawyer, former college law instructor, and daughter of the state's first Independent governor, she now serves as a Probate Judge in Waldo County.

1. **Meeting Maine voters at public events.** No matter the party, most are gracious and grateful that a candidate is reaching out to them. It's like entering the Empire Falls Diner in Richard Russo's book – Mainers are characters and everyone around knows their idiosyncrasies, but only the moment matters.

2. **Mentors.** My parents and the five kids piled into the family station wagon, and went to a speech by President John F. Kennedy three weeks before his assassination. I was young when Margaret Chase Smith became the first woman elected to both the US House and Senate. I had my picture taken with one governor. Then, my father, the post-Watergate outsider, campaigned his way into the governor's office as the state and country's first Independent governor. Unbeknownst to Democrat George Mitchell who called to concede at 3 am, November 6, 1974, he had bigger causes to champion.

3. **Considering public service a personal affair.** When I entered the state Senate, I was shocked to see many elected officials accounted mostly to lobbyists — chit-chatting in the hallways, at after-hours receptions, and even in legislative chambers as votes were occurring. I soon said lobbyists could only speak to me at hearings as I wanted constituents to hear what was said. The personal political cost taught me an invaluable lesson about the grit it takes to serve with integrity.

4. **Setting a calm, respectful tone** for discourse on emotional issues that could easily dissolve into acrimonious, go-nowhere debates by politicians looking to see themselves on the evening news. Two such issues were death with dignity and late-term abortion. As Senate Chair of the Judiciary Committee, I tried to make respectful opening statements, acknowledging the strongly-held, opposing views of my colleagues, hoping to set the tone for civil discourse.

5. **Being treated to kids** who were given a day off from school to visit the Statehouse. The halls are long and wide, so we could race from one end to another, and show kids what a public servant is called upon to do in a day—what JFK called "God's work."

Did you know. . .

MAINE'S DEBT BURDEN

- Tax-supported debt per capita is $618. The national median is $889.
- Tax-supported debt as a percentage of personal income is 1.9 percent. The national median is 2.6 percent.

Source: Moody's

TAKE5 FIVE MAINE STATE HOUSE FACTS

1. The cost of the building, completed in 1832, was originally estimated at $80,000 but the final bill totaled $139,000.

2. It was designed by world-renowned architect Charles Bulfinch and built out of granite hauled from Hallowell quarries.

3. Between 1909 and 1910, the House endured some major remodeling – almost all the old buildings were demolished, save the portico and the front and rear walls. The cost of these renovations came in at $350,000.

4. The dome of the House is surmounted by the draped female figure of Wisdom, made of copper overlaid with gold.

5. In 1991, a local citizen with a metal detector came across what is thought to be the original time capsule embedded in the cornerstone beside the fifth step of the original seven-step stairway to the main entrance. It has yet to be opened.

PERCENT OF PERSONAL INCOME

Maine state government spent slightly more as percent of personal income than most New England states in 1997 and 2010.

	1997	2010
Connecticut	18.1	17.9
Massachusetts	20.9	21.0
Maine	23.9	25.1
New Hampshire	17.4	17.7
Rhode Island	21.7	24.4
Vermont	24.0	25.5

Sources: Bureau of Economic Analysis, US Census Bureau

POLITICAL SALARIES

	Average state salary	Average local government salary
Connecticut	$59,162	$52,247
Massachusetts	$54,723	$48,776
Maine	$43,590	$35,568
New Hampshire	$44,309	$38,794
Rhode Island	$54,337	$52,272
Vermont	$47,828	$36,846

Source: US Census Bureau

Did you know. . .

. . . that Governor Jame B. Longley used his power of veto more than all Maine governors combined?

SUMMER HOMES

The picture-postcard town of Kennebunkport has assumed a national profile as a result of being the location of the summer residence of one of America's most successful political families. The Bush Compound, located on Walker Point, has been in the family for more than 100 years,

Plaisted

"I think that the best plan would be to burn down the shacks with all their filth," Governor Frederick Plaisted was quoted as saying in a newspaper account after visiting Malaga Island, a fishing community off Phippsburg. The community was poor and its inhabitants were of mixed race; mostly descendants of freed slaves, Irish, Scottish, and Portuguese immigrants.

"Certainly, the conditions there are not creditable to our state, and we ought not to have such things near our front door, and I do not think that a like condition can be found in Maine, although there are some pretty bad localities elsewhere."

Plaisted ordered the residents evicted by July 1, 1912 and had all buildings removed, bodies disinterred and reburied elsewhere, and the school building moved to another island. Seven island residents were committed to the Maine School for the Feeble Minded by order of a judge, and authorities threatened to send the rest of the inhabitants there if they failed to leave the island as ordered.

Historians say a number of factors influenced the times when these events took place. One was the eugenics movement that had taken hold in the US, which held that blacks were inferior; a rise in tourism and an accompanying interest in the purchase of island summer homes by vacationers; and a rising middle-class that believed in self-improvement and moral reform.

All these factors caused a culture clash between the upscale whites, such as Plaisted and the others who toured Malaga with him, and the poverty and color of the islanders.

The 41-acre Malaga is now owned by the Maine Coast Heritage Trust and preserved as open space. Archeologists from the University of Southern Maine are doing research on the island.

and pictures of visiting world leaders coming to visit the Bush family here have been seen around the world.

Located on Campobello Island, in Passamaquoddy Bay, New Brunswick, Canada, Roosevelt Campobello International Park is connected by bridge to Lubec, Maine. The park is administered by a joint United States-Canadian commission, and its central attraction, of course, is the former summer home of US President Franklin D. Roosevelt. Roosevelt was stricken with poliomyelitis while vacationing here in 1921.

Muskie

In 1954, Edmund Sixtus Muskie from Rumford was elected the first Democratic Maine governor since 1937 and only the fourth since 1883. Until Muskie, Maine had been so staunchly Republican it was one of only two states (the other was Vermont) to vote against Franklin D. Roosevelt in 1936.

In 1958, he defeated an incumbent to win a US Senate seat by a huge margin. He was one of the first senators who worked to clean up the environment and was reelected three more times with more than 60 percent of the vote. In 1972, Muskie was considered the frontrunner for his party's presidential nomination, but lost in part over two issues – a phony letter published in a New Hampshire newspaper in which Muskie allegedly refers to French-Canadians as "Canucks," as well as reports that he cried during a speech when defending his wife against attacks in the same paper. It was later learned the "Canuck" letter was one of Nixon's dirty tricks and Muskie claimed his face was wet with snowflakes during the speech.

In 1980 President Jimmy Carter chose Muskie as his Secretary of State and awarded him the Presidential Medal of Freedom in 1981. In 1987, Muskie served on the "Tower Commission" investigating President Ronald Reagan's administration's role in the Iran-Contra scandal.

venues in most Maine small towns, many bands have emerged from rural areas and play at dances, town hall concerts, and country and bluegrass music festivals around the state.

Maine has produced several famous home-grown musicians, including singer-songwriters Gordon Bok and Dave Mallett. One of Mallett's

and ongoing pain and loss of stamina resulting from the accident, King said he would retire; however, since then he has produced several new books.

In 2003 King received the National Book Foundation's Medal for Distinguished Contribution to American Letters. While he's an international literary star, he's not the only one in his family with talent. His wife, Old Town Maine-born Tabitha King, is the author of seven published novels and a work of nonfiction. Five of the novels take place in the fictitious Maine town of Nodd's Ridge.

In May 1987, Stephen and Tabitha were awarded Honorary Doctorates of Humane Letters from their alma mater, University of Maine in Orono. They are also philanthropists, having started two foundations; the Stephen and Tabitha King Foundation and the Barking Foundation. Their charitable efforts have built a baseball field in Bangor (he's a big Red Sox fan) and helped rebuild the Bangor Public Library.

The couple have three children, two sons—also writers—and a daughter. One son opted not to trade on the famous name. Joe Hillstrom King uses the pen name Joe Hill, an homage to the famed labor leader for whom he was named. Hill writes novels and comics, while younger brother Owen King is primarily a short story writer.

Like L.L. Bean, Stephen King draws fans from afar. The Greater Bangor Convention and Visitors Bureau offers bus tours of King related sites, and Betts bookstore on Hammond Street and Bookmarcs on Harlow Street specialize in the scare master's work.

11 albums included "The Garden Song," a tune which has been recorded more than 150 times and in several languages. Mallet's folky songs have been recorded by the likes of Emmylou Harris, Pete Seeger, John Denver and the Muppets. His latest production is *The Fable True*, based on 22 stories from Henry David Thoreau's 1864 book *The Maine Woods*.

You Can't Get There From Here

"Have you lived here all your life?" Answer: "Not yet." It's short and old, but it's a good example of dry Maine "Down East" humor.

A longer example is a classic joke immortalized by the team that called themselves Bert and I: A lobsterman loses his wife overboard in bad weather. He doesn't find her body for a week. When he hauls her up, many lobsters are clinging to her corpse; another lobsterman asks what he did with her. The widower tells him that considering the high price lobsters are fetching, he's going to set her again.

Fictional fishermen Bert and I were really two Yale students, Marshall Dodge and Bob Bryan, who were not from Maine, but who both loved Maine storytelling. In 1957, they recorded some of their stories just for fun. They made a few copies for friends, then a few more, then the Bert and I record became a phenomenal hit. Dodge and Bryan made several other hit records and spawned imitators, putting the national spotlight on Maine humor; a slow, building story-telling kind of humor. Many Bert and I stories poked sly fun at city folk visiting Maine without a clue or a concern about the native country folk who regularly get the best of the slickers.

"You can't get there from here," is the punch line to one of their classic stories, "Which Way to Millinocket?"

When Marshall Dodge died in 1982, Boothbay native Tim Sample recorded four Bert and I albums with Bryan. Sample has a full-time

Crime and Punishment

CRIME LINE

1632: The infamous pirate known as Dixie Bull stops by to sack the Pemaquid region, which is the center of the lucrative fur trade. He makes off with about $2,500 worth of goods.

1636: The first death penalty statutes are recorded in the New World. Among the offenses punishable by death are idolatry, witchcraft, blasphemy, murder, assault, sodomy, adultery, rape, perjury, and rebellion. Statutes are listed in "The Capitall Lawes of New-England."

1720: Noted pirate Edward Teach, aka Blackbeard, allegedly honeymoons on the Isles of Shoals.

1720-1725: York Gaol is built and serves as a prison until 1879. Today it is a National Historic Landmark.

1724: Father Sebastian Rasles, a French Jesuit, is killed by Massachusetts militia at an Indian village at Norridgewock, later Madison.

1766: A mob in Falmouth (Portland) seizes a cargo of sugar and prevents capture of runaway seamen in protest of British regulations; a precursor to the Revolutionary War.

1789: The Judiciary Act of 1789, passed September 24, organizes Maine, a part of Massachusetts, as one judicial district and authorizes one judgeship for the US district court.

1801: The Judiciary Act of 1801, passed February 13, reorganizes the federal judiciary into six circuits, includes the District of Maine in the First Circuit, and requires three circuit judges to hold two annual sessions of the US circuit court in the District of Maine.

1802: The Judiciary Act of 1801 is repealed and the judicial organization in effect before 1801 is restored.

1808: Ebenezer Parker of Cumberland becomes Maine's first officer to be killed in the line of duty.

1808: In April, authorities try to arrest Daniel Brackett for debt. He is the leader of a band calling themselves "White Indians," who are known for terrorizing deputies who came for them, often killing, cooking, and eating their horses. He and his pals refuse to pay the taxes and Brackett flees to upstate New York.

1820: Shortly after Maine becomes a state, a new law assigns the District of Maine to the First Circuit and requires two US circuit courts to be held in the district every year.

1824: Legislature establishes the Maine State Prison in Thomaston. This maximum-security prison houses women prisoners as well, although they are kept separate from the men.

1844: African-American Macon B. Allen of Portland practices law in Maine without a license. A year later, he is admitted to the Massachusetts bar, the first African-American to gain that distinction.

Murder of Paul Chadwick in Malta, Maine

Two hundred years have passed since the murder of surveyor Paul Chadwick rocked the small farming community of Malta, later renamed Windsor, in easternmost Kennebec County. The crime signaled the climax of the so-called Malta War, an armed insurrection of local squatters who clashed with visiting constables, surveyors, and other agents of the Plymouth Company when Maine was still part of Massachusetts.

On September 8, 1809, Chadwick was attacked and shot by a group of men disguised as Indians. After he died several days later, the men were rounded up, arrested, jailed in Augusta, and indicted for murder. Following a bold threat by fellow settlers to break the "white Indians" out of jail, the militia was called out. Their trial began on November 16.

Tried before four justices of the Supreme Judicial Court were David Lynn, Jabez Meigs, Elijah Barton, Prince Cain, Nathaniel Lynn, Ansel Meigs, and Adam Pitts.

As explained in a rare 188-page book on the trial published in 1810, and in other printed sources, the defendants pleaded not guilty. On November 25, the jury agreed.

Writes George J. Varney in the 1886 "A Gazeteer of the State of Maine," "The evidence, though conclusive as to the killing by some person in the company accused, did not show whose shot caused the death of the unfortunate man; and as the public feeling was largely in favor of the accused, all were acquitted by the jury."

To appease settlers and discourage future violence, the Legislature passed a Betterment Act which attempted to clarify the landowner-tenant relationship. It took Chadwick's murder to bring about this needed change.

1851: The "Maine Law," instigated by Portland's Neal Dow, passes as part of the national Temperance movement, prohibiting the manufacture and sale of alcohol in the state; the national law passes 68 years later.

1854: The state prison is rebuilt following a fire.

1864: Addison's Henry Plummer, gold miner and sheriff, is hanged by the Vigilante Committee, reportedly because he was a leader of gold thieves

Murder of Sarah H.

One of the most sensational Maine murder cases of the 19th century centers on the strangulation of Sarah H. Meservey in her Tenants Harbor home on the snowy night of December 22, 1877. Sailor Nathan F. Hart, a neighbor of Meservey's, was convicted and sentenced to life in prison for the crime, but the case is still mired in doubt.

Did Hart wrap Meservey's woolen scarf around her neck and cause her death? Had she angered him by rejecting his advances six months before? At his 1878 trial, a jury convicted Hart, who lacked an alibi for the night of Dec. 22, of murder in the first degree. Hart narrowly escaped the hangman since Maine had abolished the death penalty.

A book published in 1882 purported to prove Hart's innocence, casting doubt on handwriting samples introduced at the trial. "An Innocent Man in a Felon's Cell" brought national sympathy for Hart, who died in state prison in 1883.

The author, handwriting expert Alvin R. Dunton, who had caused Hart to be arrested in the first place, but who had testified in court in his defense, argued that a letter found on Meservey's kitchen floor stating "I kiled her" was written not by Hart, but by Captain Albion Meservey.

In 1930 the *Rockland Courier-Gazette* added a new twist by printing a confession by Hart's counsel at the trial, Job H. Montgomery, who stated that Hart killed Meservey accidentally after burglarizing her home. When she wrestled Hart, he caught her scarf which suddenly tightened up and killed her.

credited with murdering 120 miners and dismembering their bodies. He was involved in several murders before that, but had received pardons because they were ruled self-defense; later reports say he was hanged an innocent man and was never in fact involved in the gang trade.

1875: Louis Wagner, a German fisherman, is taken to Maine State Prison where he is among the last people hanged before Maine abolishes the death penalty. He was tried and convicted for the killing of two innocent women on one of the Isles of Shoals on March 6, 1873, known in Maine lore as the Smuttynose Murders.

1876: 74-year-old Robert Trim, his 32-year-old daughter, Melissa Thayer, and her 4-year-old daughter, Josie, are murdered on Trim's farm, which is then set ablaze. Neighbor Captain Joseph Smith is tried, convicted (despite a lack of witnesses, evidence, or motive), and spends 32 years in Thomaston Prison until he is beaten to death with a pipe there in 1908.

1883: Maine rescinds a law against interracial marriage, instituted in 1820 when Maine became a state (a carryover from a 1715 Massachusetts law).

1887: After abolishing the death penalty once and reinstating it, Maine becomes the first state to abolish it twice.

1919: The Maine Correctional Center in Windham is established by the Legislature on April 4 as a medium/minimum-security facility. Originally called the Reformatory for Men, it was later named the Men's Correctional Center.

1923: Fire again claims the Maine State Prison. When the prison is rebuilt, several additional prison units dealing with special populations are added.

1930: Portland Patrolman Michael Connolly is found dead on an Eastern Prom beach, face down with his hands cuffed behind his back,

Purington Murders

Lizzie Borden, the New England spinster who was tried, and acquitted, of slaughtering her father and stepmother with an axe in 1892, had nothing on Captain James Purington. The respected farmer went berserk on the night of July 8, 1806, butchering six of his children and his wife before slitting his own throat with a razor.

The gruesome murders occurred in the Kennebec River town of Hallowell when Maine was still annexed to Massachusetts. (The murder site is now part of Augusta, the state capital.)

"In the outer room lay prostrate on his face, and weltering in his gore, the perpetrator of the dreadful deed, his throat cut in the most shocking manner, and the bloody razor lying on a table by his side," read a lurid handbill sold on local streets. In an adjoining bedroom lay Mrs. Purington, "... her head almost severed from her body and near her on the floor, a little daughter about ten years old, who probably hearing the cries of her mother, ran to her relief from the apartment in which she slept, and was murdered on her side."

Martha Purington, one of the daughters, lingered for three weeks at Johnathan Ballard's home before dying of her injuries. Oldest son James escaped the murder house and survived with minor injuries. His brother Hezekiah also survived.

Shock waves radiated throughout the quiet town following the hatchet and razor murders. Rumors circulated that James had been an abusive father and that he was confused over his religious convictions. He was said to have written a letter to his brother while anguished over his farm's poor appearance.

"... [James] informed him that on the reception of the letter he should be dead, and requesting him to take charge of his family," stated the broadside. A horde of mourners attended the funeral of Mr. and Mrs. Purington and their six children. The bloody axe and razor reportedly were buried with James. Today the family rests in unmarked graves, with the perpetrator of the crimes interred outside the common burying ground in accordance with the custom of the time.

partially buried in sand, his watch stopped at 4:08 am. The medical examiner decides he had been thrown into the water while alive and drowned, then strangely, rules the death a drowning, not a homicide. Connolly left behind a wife and five children. Reports said two prominent bootleggers were seen leaving the area where Connolly was found, but no one was ever charged.

1930s: The Bolduc Correctional Facility is built in Warren as a farm barracks for the Maine State Prison. Known as the "Prison Farm," this minimum-security facility grows to be one of the largest dairy and beef farms in Maine.

1934: Maine's prohibition of the manufacture and sale of alcohol, first passed in 1851, is repealed a year after the repeal of the Volstead Act, which imposed national prohibition in 1919.

1935: Women prisoners are moved from the Maine State Prison to the Women's Correctional Center in Skowhegan.

1937: Gangster Al Brady, at one time the FBI's Most Wanted criminal, is gunned down by G-men in the streets of Bangor.

1959: Maine Legislature passes a bill banning discrimination in public accommodations based on race, religion, and ancestry.

1969: Fire destroys many farm buildings at the Bolduc Correctional Facility in Warren, as well as its pasteurization plant. The warden closes the farm in 1970, saying the drug culture caused its demise, since experienced farmhands were becoming rare as prisoners.

Did you know. . .

. . . that 12.3 percent of all arrests in Maine are of people aged 17 and under?

1970: The youngest daughter of Brig. Gen. Peter G. Olenchuk and his wife, Ruth, vanishes 200 yards from the family's summer home in Ogunquit on August 9; she is last seen talking to an unidentified white male in his thirties in a maroon car. The body of 13-year-old Mary C. Olenchuk is found under two feet of loose hay in a Kennebunk barn, just over 10 miles from her home, 13 days later.

TAKE5 FIVE OF EMERIC W. SPOONER'S
MAINE MURDERS

Emeric Spooner, a librarian in Bucksport, is an amateur investigator who launched a website dedicated to the state's greatest unsolved or questionable mysteries. He investigates local ghost stories, paranormal events, Maine murders, writes books, and posts his evidence online.

1. *In Search of Melissa Thayer: Reinvestigating the Trim Murders*, a book, examines the evidence surrounding the brutal murders in Bucksport of Melissa Thayer, her 4-year-old daughter, and her father, Robert Trim. Captain Edward Smith was convicted, but I think the evidence points elsewhere.

2. *In Search of Sarah Ware: Reinvestigating Murder and Conspiracy in a Maine Village*, another book, examines the unsolved murder of a Bucksport woman who went missing and was found two weeks later, beheaded and decomposed.

3. *The Bangor Strangler*. Effie Macdonald, 54, a Bangor chambermaid, was raped and then strangled to death with her nylons on March 18, 1965. Effie's unsolved murder fit the pattern of the Boston Strangler murders. Witness descriptions fit Albert DeSalvo, the convicted rapist who confessed to the 13 Boston killings, but later recanted.

4. *The Purington Massacre*. On July 14, 1806, a respected farmer, Captain James Purington of Augusta, murdered his wife and six children, then killed himself.

5. *The Smuttynose Murders*. Karen Christensen and her sister-in-law Anethe were inexplicably murdered on the small island of Smuttynose in the Isles of Shoals on March 6, 1873 by their friend, German fisherman Louis Wagner.

1972: A new warden reopens the Prison Farm in Warren and converts it to a vocational-training facility for the Bureau of Corrections. Prisoners transfer from other correctional institutions for their vocational education.

1976: The Stevens School closes and women prisoners are moved to the Maine Correctional Center in Skowhegan.

Smuttynose Murders

Although Smuttynose Island is located six miles off the coast of New Hampshire, it actually belongs to the state of Maine. It got its name from fishermen who saw in the gathering seaweed the "smutty nose" of some vast sea monster.

Unfortunately what the island is most famous for is the 1873 murder of Karen and Anethe Christensen, one of whom was strangled and the other struck with a hatchet. A third woman, Maren Hontvet, managed to escape and hid on the island at a place now known as Maren's Rock.

As the only witness, Maren would point the finger at German fisherman, Louis Wagner. Wagner used to work for Maren's husband John Hontvet, and what came out at the trial was that Wagner was hanging around the Portsmouth wharf when he heard the women were alone. He knew the Hontvets were saving for a new boat, and made a decision to rob the place.

Wagner would flee to Boston, but he was quickly picked up and returned to Portsmouth. More than 10,000 people showed up, all calling for his head. In a sensational trial in Alfred, Maine, he was condemned to death by hanging. He would escape briefly one more time before being hung by the neck at Thomaston.

The case was covered by newspapers from around the world, and in the ensuing years has provided writers and filmmakers with stories and plotlines. The story of the murders was told by Celia Thaxter in her account *A Memorable Murder* and by Anita Shreve in her novel *The Weight of Water*.

Brady Gang in Bangor

Nicknamed "The Columbus Day Massacre" or "The Battle of Bangor," it was one of the strangest events ever to rattle the quiet Penobscot River town. It ended with a 1937 gun battle that splattered the blood of Public Enemy Number One Al Brady and a crony across a downtown street.

The Indiana outlaws blazed a mid-western trail that was punctuated by 150 store robberies, five bank heists, and three murders. Busting out of jail in October 1936, the trio fled to Baltimore, Maryland, and eventually to New England in September 1937. Not the brightest lights on the block, Brady, Clarence Lee Shaffer Jr., and James Dalhover boldly drove to Maine, where they believed anyone could easily buy weapons.

Driving a big stolen Buick with Ohio plates, the fugitives stopped in the capital city of Augusta where a store clerk referred them to Dakin's Sporting Goods, a popular Bangor store. On Sept. 21, after purchasing two Colt .45 pistols, with extra clips, and a box of 50 cartridges, Dalhover and Shaffer grew edgy when storeowner Shep Hurd asked for their names.

"Those fellows look like crooks to me," Hurd commented to clerk Louis LaCrosse after the two had left. When Dalhover returned to Dakin's on Oct. 5 to pick up another weapon and inquire about a tommy gun, Hurd phoned the Maine State Police, who in turn alerted the FBI.

Federal agents set their trap at Dakin's on October 12, and when the trio returned to Central Street to pick up their machine gun, the feds beat and captured Dalhover inside the store. After Shaffer fired into the store, wounding sharpshooter Walter Walsh, agents shot the 21-year-old punk to pieces. Other agents killed Brady when he exited his Buick shooting. Street pedestrians like Marion Newcomb, whose coat was pierced by a bullet, watched in horror.

"G-men Kill Brady and Pal," screamed the *Bangor Daily News*. "One of America's most widely hunted desperado trio taken alive as guns roar in heart of Bangor's business district." Dalhover was convicted of murdering State Trooper Paul Minneman and died in the Indiana electric chair in November 1938.

1977: Lila Drew's son discovers her lifeless body on the floor of her home in Masardis on the morning of March 18 when he stops by to visit. She had been bludgeoned to death with a wooden chair leg. Authorities said the homicide took place during the previous night. The retired school teacher lived alone. Her killer was never found.

1979: The Central Maine Pre-Release Center opens in Hallowell. Prisoners here participate in a work release program and on public restitution work crews. The public restitution program has provided approximately 22,000 man hours of free labor annually to citizens of the surrounding area.

1980: The Charleston Correctional Facility opens on the site of the former Charleston Air Force Station with about 30 prisoners. Today the 145 minimum/community-rated prisoners (with fewer than 3 years remaining on their sentences) improve life skills and employability through vocational training, community restitution programs, academics, counseling programs, and work release.

1980: Joyce M. McLain's partially-clothed body is found behind the high school soccer field, with her head bludgeoned. The 16-year-old East Millinocket teen's murder has never been solved, even though forensic experts have her body exhumed and find items of interest.

1982: A small farming program begins at the old Prison Farm in Warren under the direction of a part-time prison retiree. The Prison Farm program is able to provide some staples, such as potatoes and dried beans, to all state correctional facilities.

1985: The Downeast Correctional Facility, located at the former Bucks Harbor Air Force Station, opens in June, established by the Legislature in September 1984. Funds are appropriated to purchase the facility for use as a medium/minimum-security institution with a prisoner count of 148.

1988: Dennis R. Larson was extradited from Montana for a murder in Maine the year before. He was later convicted and sentenced to 50 years in the falling death of a woman he met, married and insured just weeks after running a newspaper personal advertisement. Kathy Frost Larson plunged 80 feet to her death at Otter Cliffs in Acadia National Park on Oct. 11,

Murder, She Typed

For many years, the running joke in Maine was, "Which town in Maine has the most murders?" The answer, of course, is Cabot Cove.

That's the mythical home of fictional crime writer and amateur detective Jessica Fletcher, played for 12 years by Angela Lansbury in what became the longest-running mystery show on television. The show, supposedly set in a quiet little coastal Maine town, opened with Fletcher walking near the harbor on a sunny day, in a slicker, past people cutting fish outdoors by the side of the road, on uncovered tables, in the sun. Oh, yes, and the fishing boats in the background bore a distinctly west coast style. (The outdoor scenes were actually shot in Mendocino, California.)

The Maine accents, even to non-Mainers, left a lot to be desired. To her credit, Lansbury didn't bother. A bad Maine accent is less believable than no Maine accent. But some of her "neighbors" did try—occasionally. Real Mainers tuned in to laugh uproariously as the fake Mainers either tortured the Down East speech patterns or forgot to use them at all, often in the same sentence.

Fletcher was a substitute English teacher who turned to crime writing after her husband's death, achieved national fame, but never lost touch with her old friends. Her skill with mystery plots and her inherent nosiness prompted her to interfere regularly with police inquiries. And of course, she solved the crimes.

Over the course of the show, from 1984 to 1996, she investigated the murders of more than 260 people, many of them killed in her sleepy little town of 3,560 residents (by the time the show ended, there were far fewer). In fact, the mystery term "Cabot Cove Syndrome" came to describe bodies turning up in remote places. So, no matter what you read in the Maine police statistics... Cabot Cove still holds the record.

Did you know. . .

. . . that property crimes comprise more than 95 percent of crimes committed in Maine?

1987: Police called it a plot to collect $400,000 from a life insurance policy taken out the day after the two were wed. Authorities investigated Larson after discovering he had collected insurance money when his first wife allegedly washed away in a Montana stream.

1988: In July, Sarah Cherry, a 12-year-old girl, is kidnapped from her baby-sitting job in Bowdoin, and found dead in the woods. She had been sexually assaulted, tied, strangled and stabbed in the throat and head. Her murder is Maine's most notorious modern case.

1989: Dennis Dechaine, 30 years old and a local farmer, is arrested, tried and convicted by a unanimous jury vote of killing Sarah Cherry. Since his conviction, groups throughout the state have worked tirelessly to free him, believing that he was wrongly convicted and calling for a new trial. Police believe he is guilty and say he confessed, but his defenders say police notes show he did not. A friend forms a group called Trial and Error to help him.

TAKE5 TEN SAFEST STATES
FOR MURDER (STATE PER 100,000)

1. **Maine:** 1.2
2. **South Dakota:** 1.3
3. **New Hampshire:** 1.4
4. **Iowa:** 1.6
5. **Hawaii:** 1.7
6. **Idaho:** 1.8
7. **North Dakota:** 1.9
8. **Oregon:** 1.9
9. **Massachusetts:** 2.2
10. **Rhode Island:** 2.3

Source: FBI Uniform Crime Reports

They said it

"Crime and its causes differs in Maine from other states. We have but little organized crime, such as there is elsewhere, where they have organizations as perfect as in any other business. I believe the facts will bear me out in the statement that there is less Crime in this State, according to population, than any other state in the Union, with possibly one exception. The common belief is that Intemperance is the prime cause of all crime in this State."

– "Intemperance as a Factor in Crime in Maine,"
The Maine Historical Magazine, 1895

1989: A multipurpose male and female housing unit opens in May at the Maine Correctional Center in Windham.

1992: Maine law-enforcement officers are required to report hate crimes separately. Hate crimes are defined as those that "manifest evidence of prejudice based on race, religion, sexual orientation, or ethnicity." They are also reported to the FBI. In 1995, the reported number of hate crimes in Maine was 76, with 97 victims and 117 offenders. The majority of the crimes involve race.

1992: A new maximum-security facility opens in Warren to house 100 of the most violent criminals from the Maine State Prison, colloquially called the "Super Max."

Did you know. . .

. . . that in 2002, Harvey Taylor threatened to sue the sheriff's department in Penobscot County, blaming one of its detectives for the loss of some of his toes? Taylor, a convicted sex offender wanted in Florida, fled into the Maine woods to escape from police. Taylor spent three nights in the woods where his toes were frostbitten. Following his arrest, he said if the detective chasing him had found him earlier, his toes would have been saved!

2000: When James Rodney Hicks, then 49, was sentenced to 55 years in prison in Texas for the robbery and assault of a 67-year-old woman in Lubbock, he confessed to three murders in Maine in order to serve his time in a Maine prison rather than Texas. Hicks had been convicted in 1984, sentenced to 10 years and served six in the Maine State Prison for killing his first wife, Jennie, 23, who disappeared in 1977. Since her body had not been found, he was convicted of fourth-degree murder. Before his conviction, police had investigated but found insufficient evidence to link him to the disappearance of Jerilyn Towers, 34, of Newport. After his release in 1990, he was suspected in the disappearance of another woman he lived with, Lynn Willette, 40, of Orrington. Again, police lacked sufficient evidence for his arrest. The deal he made in Lubbock was to lead authorities to the bodies of his Maine victims. His first wife and Towers were found buried 100 feet apart next to his childhood home in Etna. Willette's remains were found in concrete buckets near a road in Aroostook County. All bodies had been dismembered.

2002: A new Maine State Prison opens in February in Warren, not too far from the historic Thomaston site. It is a maximum-security facility with a consistent population of about 900 prisoners. The old prison is demolished.

2002: A new women's unit (estimated capacity of 70) opens on July 25 at the Maine Correctional Center in Windham.

Did you know. . .

. . . that Michael Skakel, cousin of the Kennedy clan, was a student at a Maine school in 1975 when he murdered his neighbor in Connecticut? Skakel and Martha Moxley were both 15 when she was bludgeoned to death with a golf club that belonged to the Skakel family. He was enrolled at the Elan School, a boarding school for troubled youth in Poland, Maine. Skakel was tried and convicted of the murder 25 years later.

2002: A former ATF officer writes a 450-page book, *Human Sacrifice*, supporting Dechaine's claims, alleging police failed to look for other suspects.

2005: The Maine legislature votes down by 85 – 51 a bill to allow a new trial for Dechaine. His defense lawyers back off a retrial motion based on DNA because they cannot meet Maine's strict requirements for new trials. Testing shows DNA under Cherry's fingernails came from a man not Dechaine.

Maine's Most Public Hate Crime

On July 7, 1984, Charles O. Howard, a 23-year-old gay man, was walking down a Bangor street with a friend. Three teenage boys followed the pair, taunting Howard for being gay and screaming homophobic epithets.

The trio of teens caught up with the men and threw Howard over the State Street Bridge into the Kenduskeag Stream, even though he told them repeatedly that he couldn't swim. His friend, Roy Ogden, escaped and pulled a fire alarm. Rescue workers found Howard's body several hours later. Tried as juveniles, the teens were convicted and sentenced to the Maine Youth Center.

Howard's death produced a lot of action on behalf of tolerance and inspired a few literary efforts; Edward Armstrong's book, *Penitence: A True Story*, Bette Greene's novel *The Drowning of Stephan Jones*, and Mark Doty's poem "Charlie Howard's Descent." The Bangor City Council approved the building of a monument in Howard's memory to be placed near the site of his death, and residents formed the Charles O. Howard Memorial Foundation to raise money for the granite marker. The Maine Lesbian/Gay Political Alliance (MLGPA) was founded in response to the Howard murder, now known as EqualityMaine.

The murder also inspired Bangor literary giant Stephen King to describe a similar event in the beginning of his novel *It*, in which three homophobic teens throw an openly gay man, Adrian Mellon, over a bridge and into the Kenduskeag, where he is killed by the monster Pennywise.

2006: A cook is arrested for the grisly murders of four people at a bed-and-breakfast in Newry. Christian Nielsen, 31, who worked at a nearby inn, started his four-day Labor Day weekend spree by killing a man staying at the same B&B, and later killed the woman who owned the place, her daughter, and the daughter's friend. He dismembered the man, tried to burn his body, and left it in the woods nearby. The women were found at the house. No motive was ever discovered.

2007: The Women's Reentry Center in Bangor opens in November to give women the skills and experience to transition from state correctional facilities into their home communities. The center houses up to 38 women.

2009: Maine solves its first crime using Facebook; on February 17, three weeks after posting surveillance photos from an Auburn hotel's cameras on the police department's Facebook page, Auburn police arrest three teenagers for trashing a hotel spa. The teens were identified by Facebook crimestoppers.

2009: Dechaine gets a boost when famed defense attorney F. Lee Bailey decides to work on his case. Bailey was one of O.J. Simpson's "Dream Team" and worked on the trials of Sam Sheppard, Patty Hearst, and Albert DiSalvo (the alleged "Boston Strangler").

Did you know. . .

. . . that vanity can lead to arrest? A 21-year-old Portland man popped a blue light on the roof of his pickup truck and pulled over a car—the wrong man, as it turned out. The car's occupant, an off-duty federal agent, left his car and walked toward the truck. The truck's driver pulled a shotgun, threatened the agent, then thought better of it and roared away. Sadly for him, his vanity plate of ACE HI was easy for the agent to remember. Police went directly to his home to arrest him for impersonating an officer, among other charges.

2010: A Maine jury on Friday, June 26, 2010, convicted, Darlene George, of Old Orchard Beach and her brother, Jeffrey Williams, of murder and conspiracy for killing the woman's husband and trying to make it look like a home invasion.

2014: Crime in Maine dropped by 14.9 percent, the largest drop in the 40 years since the state has compiled statistics. However, that year also proved a cautionary tale about social media and crime. One man wanted for burglary in central Maine avoided arrest for stealing two stoves until he revealed his whereabouts on Snapchat. Another man was convicted of a murder he committed in 2013 when he used a phony Facebook page to lure a 15-year-old girl to her death in a failed attempt to look like a hero. Kyle Dube, 21, kidnapped the girl and imprisoned her, planning to "rescue" her later. She was found after an 8-day search, dead from asphyxiation.

CRIME IN MAINE

The Index Crime Rate (serious crimes selected by the Uniform Crime Reporting System for comparison purposes among states) in Maine is 36 percent lower than the national average, according to the FBI. The average rate for Index Crimes committed in Maine over the last 10-year period per 1,000 residents was 26.83, compared to the national rate per 1,000 of 41.64. Maine cleared 28 percent of the cases.

Murders in Maine averaged 20 per year in the same decade for a rate of 0.01 per 1,000, while across the US, the rate was 0.06. Robberies averaged 287 for 10 years. Maine's rate of robberies per 1,000 averaged a mere 0.22 compared to the national rate per 1,000 of 1.51.

Did you know. . .

. . . that Portland hired its first African-American police chief on March 3, 2009? He is James Craig, a 28-year veteran of the Los Angeles Police Department.

TAKE**5** FIVE MOST POPULAR
ITEMS MAINE THIEVES STEAL

1. Motor Vehicles (27 percent)
2. Money (14 percent)
3. Jewelry, Precious Metals (11 percent)
4. TVs, Radios, VCRs, Cameras (4 percent)
5. Office Equipment (3 percent)

Source: Government of Maine

DECLINING CRIME

In the last 10 years, Maine's Index Crime percentage declined, mirroring the national rate. Researchers say the following contributed to the decline:

- Changing demographic patterns – such as fewer people in the 18-35 age group, who are generally the most frequent offenders
- The incarceration of violent offenders

CRIME BY THE HOUR

The crime clock average in Maine reflected the following:

- Violent crimes: 1 every 5 hours, 38 minutes
- A murder every 17 days, 9 hours, 9 minutes
- A rape every 22 hours, 17 minutes
- A robbery every 25 hours, 6 minutes
- An aggravated assault every 11 hours, 3 minutes
- Property crimes: 1 every 16 minutes, 18 seconds
- A burglary every 78 minutes, 43 seconds
- A larceny every 21 minutes, 51 seconds
- A motor vehicle theft every 6 hours, 57 minutes
- An arson every 36 hours, 3 minutes

COMPARING CRIMES

Arrests for violent crimes and property per 100,000 population.

State	Total, All Classes	Violent Crime	Property Crime
Maine	4,254	63	564
New Hampshire	4,111	41	213
Vermont	2,289	53	193
United States	4,695	205	558

Source: Maine Statistical Analysis Center

CRIME BY COUNTY

Lincoln is the safest county in Maine with a crime rate of 16.97 per 1,000, with Aroostook coming in second with 17.12. The counties having the most crime are Penobscot at 33.57 and Piscataquis at 32.19.

Source: Government of Maine

MAINE CRIME CLEARANCE

A crime index offense is cleared when a law enforcement agency has identified the offender, there is enough evidence to charge him, and he is taken into custody. There are also a few exceptional circumstances when some elements beyond law enforcement control precludes formal charges against the offender, including, but not limited to, the suspect committing suicide, the offender dying after making a confession on his deathbed, the offender being killed by law enforcement officials, or another jurisdiction refusing to extradite the offender.

Did you know. . .

. . . that Stephen King's novella *Rita Hayworth and the Shawshank Redemption* was the basis for the 1994 movie, *The Shawshank Redemption*? The prison in the story was modeled loosely after the old Maine State Prison, but the plot is fiction. The film, starring Tim Robbins and Morgan Freeman, didn't make a big splash at the box office on its release, but enjoyed critical acclaim and has proven to have long-lasting popularity on cable and DVD. It is now ranked as one of the best films of all time.

Offense	Percent Cleared
Murder	95.2
Forcible rape	43.5
Robbery	41.0
Aggravated assault	72.4
Burglary	20.7
Larceny theft	29.8
Motor vehicle theft	32.9
Arson	28.0

Source: Government of Maine

POLICE EMPLOYMENT DATA

Statewide there are 2,281 full-time sworn law-enforcement officers, representing a ratio of 1.73 officers per 1,000 population. Nationally, the average rate per 1,000 was 2.4.

Maine State Trooper recruits earn a yearly salary of $34,528.60 while in the Academy. After graduation from basic law enforcement training, troopers receive salary of $36,025.60 which progresses to a seniority level of $46,592.00.

Source: Maine State Police

CAPACITY AND CENSUS
(MALE PRISONERS AS OF FEBRUARY 2009)

State Correctional Facility	Total Beds	Occupied Beds
Maine State Prison	914	872
Bolduc Correctional Facility	180	176
Maine Correctional Facility	480	486
Downeast Correctional Facility	140	145
Charleston Correctional Facility	135	131
Central Maine PreRelease Ctr.	55	52
Total Male Prisoners in all facilities including county jails	2,063	1,998

Native Americans

Evidence of the Paleo-Indians in present day Maine goes back more than 10,000 years. They disappeared from the region after about 500 years, but centuries later another group of Paleo-Indians visited briefly, followed by a variety of "Archaic" people.

The coastal Red Paint people's burial sites date from 3,800 to 5,000 years ago. By the 1400s, more than 20,000 Indians in three separate ethnic groups lived in what is present day Maine. The Armouchiquois lived in southern Maine, the Etchemin in mid- to northern Maine, and the Abenaki in the interior and western sections. The Etchemin became today's Maliseet and Passamaquoddy tribes. The Souriquois, who lived mainly east of the St. John River in New Brunswick, became today's Micmac.

Around 1600, Native Americans in Maine had their first contact with European settlers, and by 1620, fishing and trading were established. Maine's Indian history sadly mirrors that of most Native Americans after the arrival of European settlers. It is marked by disease, war, disenfranchisement, and to a large degree, destruction of a way of life.

The "Great Dying" occurred between 1616 and 1619, when the first of several epidemics caused by contact with Europeans killed entire coastal groups—up to 95 percent of Maine Indians from Penobscot Bay to Cape

Cod were wiped out. The diseases are believed to have been plague, small-pox, cholera, measles, hepatitis, and whooping cough.

Around 1700, the four remaining tribes, (Penobscot, Passamaquoddy, Maliseet, and Micmac), joined together in a council known as the Wabanaki ("People of the Dawn") Confederacy to protect themselves from increasingly aggressive European colonization. The alliance was successful in preventing wars among the tribes.

FIRST RECORDED EUROPEAN-NATIVE AMERICAN CONTACT

It is possible Englishman John Cabot was the first European to set foot on Maine soil when he sailed through the Gulf of Maine in 1498. But Italian explorer Giovanni da Verrazzano was the first explorer to leave a clear record of such contact when he searched the Atlantic seaboard for a passage to the Orient in 1524.

Verrazzano also left us the first recorded contact between Europeans and Native Americans in Maine. Verrazzano's ship made landfall at Bald Head in Eastern Casco Bay to trade with natives. The two parties exchanged a few items, but Verrazzano wasn't taken with the locals. "We found them lacking of courtesy," he wrote. The encounter ended in what may be the first recorded mooning in the history of the New World: "When we had nothing more to exchange . . . the men made all the signs of scorn and shame that any brute would make . . . such as showing their buttocks and laughing immoderately."

TODAY

Today, Maine's Native Americans have many initiatives underway to help preserve their culture and language for future generations. Maine's Indians live all over the state, but those choosing to live in Indian communities live on three reservations.

They said it

"*Long ago, the Indians were always fighting against each other. They struck one another bloodily. There were many men, women and children who alike were tormented by these constant battles. It seemed as if all were tired of how they had lived wrongly. The great chiefs said to the others, 'Looking back from here the way we have come, we see that we have left bloody tracks. We see many wrongs. And as for these bloody hatchets, and bows, arrows, they must be buried forever.' Then they all set about deciding to join with one another in a confederacy.*"

– From a Passamaquoddy narrative at the formation of the Wabanaki Confederacy

PASSAMAQUODDY TRIBE

The Passamaquoddy name refers to catching fish with a hand held spear. Passamaquoddies would travel to the coast in summer to fish, hunt, and plant corn, returning inland in the winter to hunt big game like moose and deer. Passamaquoddy Indians are known for their fine beadwork and beautifully woven baskets.

The Passamaquoddy tribe has 3,369 members with 2,005 at Pleasant Point, near the Canadian border, and 1,364 at Indian Township. They are governed by a joint tribal council with a Tribal Governor (Sakom).

PENOBSCOT NATION

Pronounced Puh-NOB-scott, Penobscot means "the place where the rocks open out." They fished the Penobscot River and were also known for their birch bark canoes. Penobscot Indian artists are best known for their basket-weaving, quill work, and bead work. Their baskets were originally made from birch bark but ash splint became more popular and has remained so for the past 200 years. Of the 3,000 members of the Penobscot Nation, or "penawahpskewi," in Maine, about 562 live at the reservation on Indian Island in Old Town.

MICMAC TRIBE

Pronounced MICK-mack. Micmac originally derived from a word that meant "my friends." Most now live on the Canadian side of the border. Micmac Indian artists were especially skilled at porcupine quillwork and also did traditional beadwork and basketweaving. The Micmac version of the well-made birch bark canoes had a distinct upward curve in the middle.

In 1991, the 1000-member Aroostook Band of Micmacs in Presque Isle finally achieved federal recognition with the passage of the Aroostook Band of Micmacs Settlement Act. They also have no reserve.

MALISEET TRIBE

The Micmac used the word Maliseet to mean "talks imperfectly." The Maliseet lived on both sides of the American/Canadian border; today most live in New Brunswick and Quebec. Early Europeans thought Maliseets made the most beautiful beadwork of all the American Indians.

The 800-member Houlton Band of Maliseets does not have a reserve, but as part of the Association of Aroostook Indians, has access to federal and state programs. They have been recognized as a government by the US since 1980 with tribal offices in Littleton.

Did you know. . .

. . . that in 1853, Henry David Thoreau took a train to Greenville, and canoed from there to Bangor by way of 2-mile long portages? His guide was Penobscot Indian Joe Attean, whose name is the same as Attean Lake in Jackman. The name probably comes from the French name Etienne, or Steven, showing how the three cultures, Native, French, and English, combined. When Thoreau was on his deathbed, dying at age 44 of tuberculosis, his final words were "moose" and "Indian." Apparently his time spent hiking through Maine with Penobscot Indians made a great impression.

ABENAKI TRIBE

Pronounced AH-buh-nah-kee. It means "people of the dawn," true to their eastern location. Original natives of Maine, New Hampshire, and Vermont, many Abenaki moved across the border into Canada when European colonists arrived on Maine shores. Two Abenaki bands live on reservations in Canada but the 100 or so families of Abenaki are not recognized by the US government. Many Abenaki continue to live in New England as part of the general population. The Abenaki especially considered dogs an important part of their family, particularly in the winter, and sometimes used them as pack animals.

Crossing the Color Barrier

Before Jackie Robinson became the first African-American in major league baseball in the 1940s, Louis Sockalexis, a Penobscot Indian who grew up on Indian Island, signed with the Cleveland Spiders in 1897. Sockalexis was the first Native American to join the major leagues. Often called "Sock," he compiled a batting average of .338, hit eight triples, and stole 16 bases in his first 60 games for the Spiders.

Sockalexis was born on the Penobscot Indian reservation in Old Town on October 4, 1871. According to local lore, Sockalexis would exercise by hurling baseballs 600 feet across the Penobscot River. When he played for the College of the Holy Cross and Notre Dame, one of his home runs reportedly went through a window of the Brown University Chapel and continued another 600 feet. An outfield throw, measured by two Harvard professors, went 414 feet.

But Sockalexis was fighting a losing battle with alcoholism. In his first season with the Spiders, he jumped out the second floor of a brothel, hurting his leg. He played for two more seasons, but his performance declined. At 27, he went down to the minor leagues as his alcoholism continued to grow worse. By 1906 Sockalexis returned to Indian Island where he bided time running a ferry across the Penobscot River, coaching Penobscot youths, and serving as an umpire in the Maine league. He died at age 42.

TAKE5 STEVE CARTWRIGHT'S FIVE
GREAT MAINE INDIANS

Steve Cartwright is a Maine journalist who spent five years as editor of an inter-tribal newspaper for Maine's Wabanaki Alliance. He has also worked for various daily and weekly newspapers around the state, and is now a freelance writer. Cartwright lives with his family in the coastal town of Waldoboro.

1. **Wayne Newell** is "Mr. Language" for generations of Passamaquoddy children who now learn at least the basics of their native language in reservation schools. Fluent himself, Newell was the first to introduce the teaching of Passamaquoddy in schools run by Catholic nuns who for decades forbade it. Newell managed to do this gracefully, and with humor. He is a beacon among his people and he has served his state, as well, as the first tribal member to serve on the University of Maine board of trustees. He holds a master's degree from Harvard—another first for a Passamaquoddy—and has lectured widely.

Newell serves on his tribal council, has served on Maine/Indian Tribal State Commission, and was a key member of the Penobscot-Passamaquoddy negotiating team that worked on the 1980 Maine Indian Land Claims Settlement Act.

2. **Molly Jeanette Neptune**, a Passamaquoddy, was a wise advisor to the Wabanaki Alliance newspaper that I edited. She learned the fine art of basketry, making breathtakingly fine and colorful baskets of various shapes and sizes from split brown ash and sweetgrass. The smell of that grass reminds me of Molly's sweetness, her love of children, her generosity with whatever she had, no matter how little that might be. I am fortunate to have a wedding basket Molly gave to my wife and me; she reminds me, without a trace of arrogance or hostility, that we non-Indians have a lot to learn about living in balance—with each other and with the natural environment.

3. **Senabe** had another name, Ronald Francis. Senabe was a respected traditional Penobscot medicine man and craftsman, carving intricate clubs and walking sticks. He enjoyed people, Indians and non-Indians alike, but he also enjoyed something that has destroyed many native

people: alcohol. So when you stopped by his tiny, ramshackle house on Indian Island in the Penobscot River, you never knew if he would be drunk or sober. Toward the end, you knew. Finally, the booze killed him, and the Penobscot Nation lost a valuable member, a man with a knowledge of healing powers. We could speculate on why he had to die this way. It is not easy growing up when you're considered a second-class citizen, when the message is, "Indians need not apply." I have a walking stick that he carved, and the memory of meeting someone caught between two cultures—worlds apart.

4. **Margaret Nicholas** lived to be 102. And she was tough. And could she dance. I remember being invited into her kitchen. She must have trusted me, for although Catholic like most of her people, she also believed in the Little People, something with deeper roots in tribal culture. One tribal member told me, "The English took our land, the French (Catholic missionaries) took our souls." Finally, after a couple of cups of coffee, Mother Nicholas, as the tribe called her, decided she would show me proof that the Little People, mischievous counterparts to us, really exist. She darted into another room and returned holding a miniature, perfectly formed steel anvil. "The Little People left it," she told me. Nobody took Margaret's soul.

5. **Donald Sanipass** is an extraordinary basket weaver from the Micmac tribe. When I visited him in a very modest house near Presque Isle, Maine, he and his Micmac wife Maryanne could not have been more welcoming. Donald welcomed my wife and me and insisted we stay the night with them, although we could see this family had little to spare. David is now an accomplished maker and player of Indian flutes, and he played for the dedication of an Indian museum in Bar Harbor. His son Donald is a photographer, self taught, and his art work is at once simple and very moving. His photos speak of a spirit that understands its place in nature, in the circle of life. Donald also serves as a leader of the Micmacs in his area, a group that along with Maliseets fought and won federal recognition as a tribe, making them eligible for land claim funds and health and other services.

LANGUAGE

The Passamaquoddy language is spoken by about 300 tribe members, more than any other Maine Indian language. Passamaquoddy and Maliseet are both dialects of the Algonquin language. The Penobscot used to speak an Abenaki-Penobscot language that has since died out, although it was written down and the Penobscot are trying to revive it. Micmac is also an Algonquin language spoken by many Canadian Micmac.

Maine's Famous Molly

Molly Spotted Elk was the stage name of a Penobscot Indian woman who took the stages of New York and Europe by storm in the early 20th century, performing native dances and singing.

She was born November 17, 1903, on Indian Island and baptized Mary Alice Nelson, the first of eight children of Philomena Solis Nelson, a Maliseet, and Horace Nelson, a future governor of the Penobscot Nation. Her mother was one of the best basket makers of her day, and her father was the first Penobscot to attend Dartmouth College.

She led an extraordinary life, starting at age 13 when she studied traditional dance to help support her family. She left Indian Island after high school for the University of Pennsylvania, where she studied anthropology and in particular other world Indian cultures. She also contributed to Dr. Frank Gouldsmith Speck's study of her tribe, *Penobscot Man: The Life of a Forest Tribe in Maine*.

Money for the study ran out, so Nelson turned to her skills at native dancing, first joining the vaudeville troupe of the famous Tex Guignan, then performing with the Schubert Theater and the Provincetown Players. By now known as "Molly Spotted Elk," she wrote her own music and made her own costumes.

She was still in her 20s when she won the lead in one of Paramount's last silent movies in 1928, "The Silent Enemy," which documented a Canadian Ojibway tribe's struggle against hunger before

PENOBSCOT ANIMAL NAMES

Alemos: dog
Ahaso: horse
Molsem: wolf
Awasos: bear
Bezo: lynx
Wokwses: fox
Azeban: raccoon
Kogw: porcupine
Megeso: eagle
Gokokhoko: owl

the Europeans arrived.

In 1931, as the American Indian representative in the ballet corps of the International Colonial Exposition, she sailed to France where she performed native dances at Fontainbleau's Conservatory of Music, then toured the continent performing for old world royalty.

After a brief return to the US where she appeared as an extra in a few Hollywood films, she went to Paris, studied at the Sorbonne, taught ballet, and married journalist John Stephen Frederic Archambaud. When World War II broke out and Archambaud, an outspoken anti-Nazi, political journalist for *Le Paris Soir*, and Red Cross Relief Director near Bordeaux, went missing, Nelson and her 6-year-old daughter, Jean, fled on foot over the Pyrenees Mountains into Portugal.

She returned to Indian Island and spent the rest of her life there, but never stopped working in the arts. She crafted Indian dolls in traditional dress, some of which are now in the Smithsonian. She wrote children's stories based on Penobscot legends, translated Penobscot into English and French and collected her diaries, notes, and a lifetime of letters. She died February 21, 1977 at the age of 73. In 1986, she was installed as a charter member of the Native American Hall of Honor in Page, Arizona. Her life was chronicled in Bunny McBride's *Molly Spotted Elk: A Penobscot in Paris* (1995).

They said it

Sips: board
Doleba: turtle

ABENAKI NUMBERS

Bazegw: one
Niz: two
Nas: three
Yaw: four
N[ô]lan *: five
Ngued[ô]z *: six
Tôbawôz: seven
Nsôzek: eight
Noliwi: nine
Mdala: ten
Sanôba: man
P[e]hanem *: woman

Did you know. . .

. . . that there's a *Wabanaki Guide to Maine; A Visitors' Guide to Native American Culture in Maine*? The spiral-bound booklet published in 2001 is a guide to museums, workshops, festivals, shops, significant landmarks, and even ancient canoe routes. Two trails are in the Acadia and Down East regions of Maine, where two of Maine's tribes live. The booklet is available from the Maine Indian Basketmakers Alliance in Old Town.

World War II Hero

Charles Norman Shay, Penobscot Nation Elder, was officially and belatedly recognized by the Maine legislature June 6, 2006 for his heroism while serving in the army during World War II. The Maine ceremony marked the 63rd anniversary of his experience on the beach at Coleville-sur-mer.

Shay was a 19-year-old combat medic when the troops landed in Normandy on D-Day. His regiment sustained about 1,000 casualties and he was awarded a Silver Star for "unselfish heroism." His citation reads: "Private Shay repeatedly subordinated personal safety for the welfare of his comrades... plunging repeatedly into the treacherous sea and carrying critically wounded men to safety."

After Normandy, Shay participated in several more battles, including the Battle of the Bulge. In 1945, his regiment captured a German bridge and he was captured when they crossed into Germany. He survived German POW camps, and returned to the Penobscot Indian reservation in 1945.

Work was scarce, so Shay re-enlisted and served as a medic in occupied Austria and later as a combat medic in the Korean War. He was promoted to Master Sergeant and awarded the Bronze Star with two Oak Leaf clusters for valor. He lived abroad for many years, including decades in Vienna with his Austrian wife.

In the mid-1990s, Shaye returned to Indian Island and inherited the house and tipi that belonged to his famous aunt Lucy Nicolar, aka Princess Watahwasso. Shay, a direct descendant of Chief Madockawando, Chief Joseph Orono, Lt. Governor John Neptune, and Joseph Nicolar—the longest-serving Penobscot Tribal Representative to the Maine Legislature in the late 19th century—was 83 years old when he was honored by Maine for his courageous and heroic service to his country, his state, and the Penobscot Nation.

PASSAMAQUODDY-MALISEET WORDS

Pesq or Neqt: one
Nis: two
Nihi: three
New: four
Nan: five
Skitap: man

TAKE5 FIVE THINGS DONALD SOCTOMAH
CARES ABOUT

Donald Soctomah is a proud member of the Passamaquoddy Tribe in Indian Township. As tribal historian and collector of oral history and artifacts, he has helped the Passamaquoddy know and respect their 12,000-year history in the region, including the language still spoken by some 300 tribal members, and the revival of traditional dancing, music, and herbal medicine. His great grandfather was a keeper of oral history for the tribe. He is a father of 10 and grandfather of 12.

1. **Introducing a bill to undo a racist tradition**. The bill passed changing the name of Maine places called "Squaw." Maine had a lot of these names across the state, but no more. The non-Indian legislature approved the measure with only a handful of Republicans in opposition. Every Democrat voted for it. "We have moved a mountain," said Vera Francis, a tribal member.

2. **Recognizing the contributions of Native American veterans**, all the way back to the American Revolution. The tribe has letters signed by George Washington seeking help in the War of Independence. President Washington wasn't disappointed, and Maine Indians have served and died for their country in every war since, although for decades they were denied full voting rights. The tribe's aid to the Revolution is one of the oldest alliances in US history.

3. **The tribe's history**. I authored two Passamaquoddy history books, and a new children's book about Chief Tomah Joseph called

Ehpit: woman
Olomuss: dog
Kisuhs: sun
Kisuhs, Nipawset: moon
'Samaqan: water
Wapi: white
Wisawi: yellow
Mqeyu or Pqeyu: red

Remember Me: Chief Tomah Joseph's Gift to Franklin Roosevelt. It tells the story of artist Joseph and the birch bark canoe he built and gave to President Franklin D. Roosevelt. It's now preserved at the Campobello Island visitor's center. The Chief used to camp on the island while FDR stayed in his spacious summer cottage and the two became friends.

4. **Concern that as tribal elders die, so does the language they spoke before learning English.** There are now dictionaries of the native tongue, but unless recordings are made, no one will really know how to pronounce words, or understand the rhythm and cadence of spoken and sung Passamaquoddy. Ten percent of native speakers died in the space of one year, so I am seeking a grant to improve teaching resources, trying to save a language from extinction. It's a lot of work.

5. **Building a museum on the reservation.** My office and the museum are in a former senior citizens center. Tribal members have donated items like a very old drum and early basket-making tools. I hope a family with a rare wampum belt will consider donating it. A 1780 drawing shows a Passamaquoddy chief wearing the belt. There are many treasures out there, but probably the richest ones are the memory banks of elders who have stories to tell, stories that are passed down from generation to the next. I hope my grandchildren will be able to pass them on, too.

Mokosewi: black
Mitsu: eat
Nomihtu: see
Nutomon: hear
Lintu: sing
Nokotomon or Macehe: leave

ANGLO-WABANAKI WARS

Six wars between the Wabanaki and the English took place as the French and English fought over territory or English settlements encroached on Indian territory. The first Anglo-Wabanaki war drove out or killed 6,000 English settlers from Wells to Pemaquid. In 1777, the French and Indian Wars ended with the Treaty of Paris which forced France to give Canada—New France & Acadia—to England. Many Wabanaki homelands were included in the swap but without the Indians' consent.

1675-1678: King Philip's War
1688-1699: King William's War
1703-1713: Queen Anne's War
1721-1726: Dummer's or Lovewell's War
1744-1748: King George's War
1755-1760: French & Indian or Seven Years War

Did you know...

. . . that the Northern Forest Canoe Trail is a 740-mile canoeing trail that extends from Fort Kent in Maine to Old Forge in the Adirondacks of New York, passing through parts of Quebec, Vermont, and New Hampshire? The trail traces the history of early travel dating from the Native Americans. Maps, books, and web-based tools are available from the web page of the organization. The trail was opened June 3, 2006 and runs the gamut from flat water on ponds and lakes, to white water on rivers.

AMERICAN REVOLUTION

Also in 1777, Eastern Maine Indians reluctantly took up arms during the American Revolution. Some Maliseets and Passamaquoddies joined British troops, but more supported colonists. There's a monument at the Pleasant Point Passamaquoddy Reservation honoring the Indians who fought with the Colonists against the British.

STATEHOOD AND STATUS

In 1820, Maine became a state and the Penobscots and Passamaquoddies became wards of the state with reservations at Indian Island, Pleasant Point, and Peter Dana Point in eastern Maine. The reservations are called "enclaves of disenfranchised citizens bereft of any special status." Unlike the federal programs for Western Indian tribes, the system of care is state-based for eastern Indians because they're considered "domesticated."

They said it

"For we are the stars. For we sing.
For we sing with our light.
For we are birds made of fire.
For we spread our wings over the sky.
Our light is a voice.
We cut a road for the soul
For its journey through death
For three of our numbers are hunters.
For these three hunt a bear.
For there never yet was a time
When these three didn't hunt.
For we face the hills with disdain.
This is the song of the stars."

— "The Stars," a Passamaquoddy Legend

MAINE'S INDIAN LAND CLAIMS SETTLEMENT

The 1980 Maine Indian Land Claims Settlement acknowledged that the US Congress never ratified treaties that took away Indian land, and awarded $81.5 million to the Passamaquoddy Tribe and the Penobscot Nation to purchase 300,000 acres of land and to establish a trust fund for tribal economic development. The act also gave the Houlton Band of the Maliseets $900,000 to buy 5,000 acres in 1992, and a separate act gave the Aroostook Band of Micmacs $900,000 to buy land.

All the Maliseet and Micmac money was put into trust funds that can be spent only for land purchases. Half the Penobscot settlement money is reserved for land purchases; the other half is held in trust, and the interest is disbursed quarterly to tribal members. Chief Richard Hamilton said the payout works out to $33 a month. Among Passamaquoddys, the bulk of the tribe's settlement money is reserved for land purchases and economic development projects. Members get annual profit-sharing from tribal businesses that amounts to less than $500 per person.

Did you know. . .

. . . that in 1973, the Penobscot Nation was one of the first Native American tribes to launch a gambling enterprise when they launched Penobscot High Stakes Bingo which is open to the public on the reservation? Several attempts have been made by Indian groups to build gambling casinos in Maine, but efforts have been rebuffed by the state. The Penobscot bingo game offers super bingo weekends every six weeks with prizes up to $250,000.

INDIAN REPRESENTATIVES OFFICIALLY RECOGNIZED

The day after President Barack Obama was sworn into office as the first African-American president, the Passamaquoddy and Penobscot tribal representatives were recognized officially by the Maine legislature for the first time in 200 years.

On January 21, 2009, the legislature added the tribal representatives' names to the official roll call board, meaning their attendance at legislative sessions will be noted and entered into the legislative record. Passamaquoddy Rep. Donald Soctomah and Penobscot Indian Nation Rep. Wayne Mitchell are the current elected representatives of the tribes.

"Our first African-American president will be a reminder to countless children in America that their potential is endless. I am very proud that when tribal children visit the State House and see the name of a tribal member on the board, they will know that they have the potential to do big things as well," Soctomah said.

"Today, I am reminded of my ancestors – my great-grandfather, my grandfather, and my uncle – who were all tribal representatives. They were forced to stand in the hallways of the State House. I am deeply appreciative to the members of the House of Representatives for this recognition," said Mitchell. Maine is the only state in the US with tribal representatives seated in the state House of Representatives. While they cannot vote in committee or on the floor of the House, they can chair committees and sponsor legislation.

Did you know. . .

. . . that conversion to Catholicism by French missionaries created strong ties between Maine Indians and the French? The ties were strengthened by intermarriage. The most famous of those marriages was between Baron St. Castin and Pidiwamiska, a daughter of Penobscot chief Madockawando.

MAINE MUSEUMS DEDICATED TO FIRST NATIONS

Abbe Museum: Features exhibits about the Wabanaki Indian Tribes of Maine in two locations. The largest one is located downtown at 26 Mount Desert Street in Bar Harbor. The other is located inside Acadia National Park at Sieur de Monts Spring off Route 3.

Penobscot Nation Museum: Devoted to Maine Native American history and art. 12 Downtown Street, Indian Island.

Maine State Museum: The place to learn about the history of the great state of Maine. Over 12,000 years of Maine history are revealed. 83 State House Station in Augusta.

Colonial Pemaquid Museum: The archaeological site of Colonial Pemaquid displays artifacts and exhibits what the 17th century fishing village was like. Includes items related to the Wawenock Indian tribe. The Fort is part of the remains of Fort William Henry. Located in New Harbor.

Weblinks

NATIVE AMERICANS' OFFICIAL WEBSITES

Penobscot Nation
www.penobscotnation.org

Passamaquoddy Tribe
www.wabanaki.com

Maliseet Tribe
www.maliseets.com

Aroostook Band of Micmacs
www.micmac-nsn.gov